Ex-Nuns:
A Study of Emergent Role Passage

MODERN SOCIOLOGY:
A Series of Monographs, Treatises, and Texts

Edited by
GERALD M. PLATT

EX-NUNS:
A Study of Emergent
Role Passage

Lucinda SanGiovanni
Seton Hall University

ABLEX PUBLISHING CORPORATION
Norwood, New Jersey
1978

*This book is dedicated to
sisters bonded by blood,
faith, and ideology
but especially to my sister
Francine E. SanGiovanni, M.D.*

Ablex Publishing Corporation
355 Chestnut Street
Norwood, New Jersey 07648

Library of Congress Cataloging in Publication Data

SanGiovanni, Lucinda F.
  Ex-nuns: A study of emergent role passage.

  (Modern sociology)
  Bibliography: p.
  Includes index.
  1. Ex-nuns—Case studies. I. Title. II. Series.
  BX4668.2.S26   301.11′3   78-18185
  ISBN 0-89391-006-6

Printed in the United States of America

Contents

Foreword

Every so often there is a perfect fit between research topic and researcher. The reader of this book will quickly experience the quality of such a match. The topic is a sensitive one, and it is treated sensitively. Consider the poignancy of one former nun's question: "How can I go out at the age of 43, get a job, and change my whole life-style?" For many of the women studied, their sense of both time and social change had been arrested when, as young girls, they had entered the convent. Upon reentry into lay life, many had to learn about sex, personal grooming, and everyday amenities, to say nothing of coping with the embarrassment of new friends or suitors who were confused about *them*. The author has an intriguing story to tell.

Yet this is an important theoretical book as well, one that conceptualizes as an emergent role passage the movement of nuns out of the convent into secular life. Their passage is "emergent" in that there were no role prescriptions for the unprecedented exodus from religious orders that occurred in the 1960s. Indeed, those who initiated the transition were active participants in shaping who they would become and how they would live in lay society.

Because of rapid changes in contemporary society, many such transitions to new roles are being created. Minorities, youth, women, the aged, homosexuals, ex-criminals, the handicapped, former mental patients, and students are all questioning their roles in society and beginning to forge new social structures and new images of themselves. Thus, as Dr. SanGiovanni points out, the understandings gleaned from these case studies of ex-nuns seem transferrable to such pervasive phenomena as delayed entry into the labor force, mid-career job changes, experimental marriages, abortion-on-demand, interrupted careers, and euthanasia. The author has chosen ex-nuns as an extreme case of an emerging transition, one that is not only self-initated but requires the relearning of love and friendship roles, work roles, even age and sex roles.

This book is organized around the three phases in a role transition: the relinquishment of what are in this instance religious roles and life-styles, the initial transition to secular life, and the acquisition of new roles and accommodation to new ways of living. The aim, the author states, is "to allow a sociological vision to enhance our understanding of how this passage was made." Extensive verbatim excerpts from the author's in-depth interviews with 20 ex-nuns succeed in capturing the subjectively experienced passages of these women, "so that we can recognize them not merely as subjects of sociological research but as individual explorers of our social terrain." The interviews are not merely perceptive reconstructions of 20 lives. They are the stuff from which theoretical insights are derived. They were initially guided by a conceptual model developed from the work of Arnold Van Gennep, Barney Glaser and Anselm Strauss, Orville G. Brim, Jr., John Clausen, and our own studies of life-course transitions. The model is carefully set out and the interviews are used to specify its components and to generate new ideas and principles. Thus, the reader of Dr. SanGiovanni's lucid account discovers how role rehearsal is accomplished in an emergent passage; how strategies for relinquishment are aided by definitions of one's self as incumbent in the anticipated new roles, not as an "ex-nun"; how new behaviors are shaped by present and future demands of others, and not determined by prior experience and early training; how the passage is not unilinear but marked by a "passage lag," which hinders but also buffers the transition; how this transition, like that of the criminal or other deviant, requires "managing" the presentation of one's biography in order to avoid stigma and stereotyping; and, finally, how there is a dynamic cycle between self and others in the use of cues for assessing performance in the new roles. One learns in detail how moving outside the boundaries of traditional roles is accompanied by confusion and fear, but also by the sense of personal freedom and authenticity. As the author puts it, "the lives of those on the frontier of social existence are a mixture of both the dark and the light sides of being different."

This work belongs in the tradition of the Rutgers program in the sociology of age. Begun when Cindy SanGiovanni was a graduate student, her exploration of emergent role transitions was part of our common endeavor toward this emergent field. The experience of the women she studied underscores a central principle of the sociology of age: that much of the process of aging is not "caused" by chronological or even biological age, but is socially prescribed. Here are chronologically adult women who were having their first dates, sexual encounters, and marriages; going for their first job interviews; earning their first salaries; establishing their first credit references; acquiring their first apartments. Moreover, the book deals effectively with several topics on which members of the original Study Group in Age Stratification continue to write: the processual nature of role transitions; the formation of new norms as not-yet-institutionalized transitions are encountered; the further social changes that are evoked because new or altered transitions have emerged. For us as a Group, it is rewarding to read and to learn from this book, and to introduce it to a wider audience.

MATILDA WHITE RILEY
*Center for Advanced Study in
the Behavioral Sciences
Stanford, California
1978*

Preface

Over the course of our lives as social beings we pass into, through, and out of many roles. Some of these personal journeys are quite familiar to us—we pass from child to teenager, from single to married, from employed to retired, from civilian to soldier. These types of role passage are fairly institutionalized in our society, guided by those accepted schedules, rituals, rules, and meanings that facilitate our movement from certain social locations into different ones.

There are other journeys between roles, however, that lack the scheduled, prescribed character of more institutionalized passages. These emergent role passages are being shaped by people who are at the social frontier of society. They are people who, singly or collectively, are creating new social locations, different role configurations, and changes in the traditional pathways to established roles. Transsexuals, the dual-career family, terrorists, the New Right, single parents, and "born-again" Christians are but a few of the social improvisations on role playing emerging in American society.

These passages into the social unknown, unprotected by institutionalized support, are accompanied by a host of poignant questions about our social identities and the kinds of roles we can play. What does it mean to be old or black or Jewish? When should we resist military induction? Should we have an abortion, a vasectomy, a sex change? Are "open-marriages" viable? When and how should we die?

The questions and issues surrounding emergent role passage are not solely a challenge to us as individuals. They also serve as an intellectual invitation to the sociologist whose task is to understand the nature of role passage both at the micro-level of the individual-in-a-role and at the higher levels of social organization.

This book is a sociological inquiry into the nature of one such emergent passage—that taken by Roman Catholic nuns who, during the late sixties and early seventies, left their convents to embark on a journey to secular roles and life-styles. In this ten-year period approximately 50,000 women relinquished their roles as nuns and their membership in religious orders. Their passage to different social identities and roles has generated important substantive and theoretical questions about the salience of religious life in modern society, the transformation of women's position in social life, and the dynamics of major role change in adulthood.

The span of time during which this exodus from religious life was taking place was also a time when many other Americans were challenging the content of established roles and social identities. The social upheavals of this decade brought about varying degrees of change in the structure of social life. The extent to which these changes will become institutionalized, be modified, or rejected outright is a question whose answer lies in the future.

The decision to explore the passage of nuns from religious to secular life was made for many reasons, both intellectual and personal. As a sociologist, I believed that this choice of subject matter provided an opportunity to examine theoretical dimensions of role passage that have yet to receive systematic attention in the discipline. Specifically, this is a passage in which we can emphasize (1) the *emergent* nature of role change, (2) the fact that *multiple,* rather than single, role transitions are involved in actual social experience, (3) the *self-initiated* and not just socially determined dimensions of role passage, (4) the phenomenon of *aging* as a process that entails expectations for role exits and entrances, and (5) the *processual* nature of a passage out of, through, and into social roles.

Personal motives also shaped my choice of this topic. Although I was never a nun, I did come from a Roman Catholic background and was interested in the dramatic changes taking place in many sectors of the Roman Catholic community in the U. S. during the post-Vatican Council II years. As a feminist, I also wanted to study a group of women who, like their secular sisters, were involved in a re-examination of their participation in roles, relationships, and institutions. There was, finally, a sense that this event was historically unique and should be studied while the opportunity afforded itself.

Thus, this is a book about emergent role passage in adult life, about nuns and former nuns, and about women. Some of the questions raised in this study are:

How did women, once committed to the role of a nun, make the decision to relinquish religious life?

What part was played by religious orders and the secular environment in influencing this decision?

How did these women intentionally prepare themselves for making the transition to secular life? Which patterns of religious behavior inadvertently became forms of "rehearsal" for leaving the convent?

How did strategies emerge for determining the manner and the timing of their leave-taking? What consequences did these strategies have for later adjustments to secular life?

Upon leaving religious life, how did these women assume such secular roles as adult, worker, friend, lover, consumer, and the like? What problems of accommodation and accountability arose for ex-nuns and how did they attempt to solve them?

What part did transitional agents and processes play during the postconvent phase of the passage? How did these factors shape subsequent acquisitions of secular roles and life-styles?

How did former nuns know their passage was completed? Which personal and social criteria emerged to signal the successful adjustment to secular society? Which social processes and arrangements had a major role in affecting the degree of adjustment that had been made?

How does an examination of this type of role passage yield insights into similar kinds of role change among adults? What are the implications of these emergent role passages for social change in American society? What demands will they make on present societal arrangements that depend on the successful allocation of people to social roles?

Since these are relatively uncharted and complex areas of sociological inquiry, I chose to do an exploratory case study of women who had left a particular religious order. Data were collected primarily through the use of intensive interviews. Exploratory case study research is one initial step in the sociological enterprise, having its unique merits and limitations. I hope that I have been sensitive to the former and conscious of the latter.

Every book is written with multiple aspirations. The two most central to me are that this book makes a contribution to the sociological understanding of emergent role passage and that, by portraying how persons experience and accomplish their movement through social locations, it adds to the list of works that celebrate the rich, dynamic improvisations of the person-in-passage.

LUCINDA SANGIOVANNI
Seton Hall University
So. Orange, N.J.

Acknowledgments

Every book has a special history and, as such, it belongs to all those who helped give it shape and content. I am most grateful to the hundreds of women, both nuns and former nuns, who shared their experiences with me and especially to those who agreed to participate in this study.

A part of my intellectual debt is reflected in the text and the references. I was also fortunate to have been a doctoral candidate at Rutgers University during the late sixties and early seventies. The scholarly stimulation of Professors Peter Berger, Harry Bredemeier, Earl Rubington, and Jackson Toby, who represent a variety of sociological perspectives, sharpened my desire to study the emerging role changes that were occurring at that time. It is to Matilda W. Riley, however, that I am most indebted. She was and remains a generous and steady source of ideas, criticism, and encouragement. I hope that this book reflects my gain from knowing her.

The following colleagues also made special contributions to the book: Ihor V. Zielyk converted me to sociology and, for more than a decade, has been a faithful friend and critic; Mary A. Boutilier challenged me in every chapter to refine my ideas and gave me the support to do so; Lynn Atwater, Philip Kayal, and Howard Robboy offered valuable assistance both professionally and personally.

The editors and staff of Ablex Publishing Corporation have been most cooperative. I am especially thankful to Lawrence Erlbaum and Jon Dahl for their confidence and enthusiasm and to Rowena Friedman for her editorial work. Anda Aistars, Beverley Andalora, Karen Kaduscwicz, and Peggy Palmere skillfully and cheerfully shared the task of typing the manuscript.

Finally, I want to thank my parents who gave both of their daughters a chance.

Ex-Nuns:
A Study of Emergent Role Passage

PART I
INTRODUCTION

1
Role Passage in Adult Life

More than a half century ago, Arnold Van Gennep's *Les rites de passage* (1908) brought to the attention of social scientists the significance and dynamics of what are now known as role passages. While he concentrated primarily on the passages that occur between age-related roles—child to adult, unmarried to married—subsequent scholarly research has extended our knowledge of different types of passages and their significance for social behavior. Anthropologists (Gluckman, 1962) have provided us with rich descriptions of the meanings and rituals that attend the major transitions necessary for group life. In psychology, seminal works such as Erik Erikson's (1950) *Childhood and Society* have underscored the salience of a life cycle model in studying the individual's passage through role crises.

In sociology, role passages have been investigated on two major levels. At the micro level of the individual-in-a-role a person is viewed as passing into, through, and out of the array of roles that make up part of the structure of a society. At this level sociologists study a range of issues. What social factors encourage an individual to assume certain roles and not others? How is preparation made for the successful performance of expectations? What influence do role partners and reference groups have on an individual's actual role performance and his or her commitment to particular roles? What factors influence the leaving of roles and the subsequent accommodation to role loss? These, and other questions, highlight the movement of persons through the roles available in a society. Well-known sociological studies of divorce, professional careers, stigma, retirement, and dying suggest the range of interest in role passage at the micro level of social life.

At the macro level society can be viewed as a composite of individuals in roles, groups, and larger aggregates located at various stages and places in the life course (Riley, Johnson, & Foner, 1972, p. 517). Historically, sociologists have indirectly raised questions about role change at this level by virtue of their extensive investigations of processes that create demands for role passages in adult life. Such processes as urbanization, industrialization, immigration, technology, and social mobility are examples of social forces that create new social locations while eroding others. Recently, more systematic attention has been given to the conceptualization of role passages as links between individual biography and social change. Through the major societal processes of socialization and role allocation we can examine the interplay between the individual-in-a-role and forces at work in the larger society. This idea involves looking at society as:

> The composite of the several but unique cohorts—at varying stages of their journey, and often traveling divergent paths; only by understanding this fact can we also recognize the differing rhythms of individual and society and the sources of tension inherent in these differences in rhythm. (Riley et al., 1972, p. 517)

At the societal level, then, role passages generate important sociological issues. How does a social system articulate the existing pool of individuals with the available role openings in the society? How much strain occurs in a society as a result of differing patterns of role passage among segments of the population? How do societal processes influence the types of roles available and the shapes these passages will take? How do role passages themselves generate social change in our society?

The bewildering variety of such passages that occur in everyday life and the complexity of sociological questions they raise demands codification of this phenomenon in order that it receives systematic investigation. To help meet this demand, Glaser and Strauss (1971) identified a number of "properties of status passage." They categorize passages according to the degree to which, for example, they are scheduled, regularized, desirable, reversible, and voluntary. Passages can differ, therefore, in terms of the degree to which any combination of these and other properties are present in a particular passage to be studied. But the situation is even more complex than this. As we look at individuals over the life course, we realize that they are involved in more than one transition at a time, thus increasing the complexity of the issues involved in a single role passage. That is, the typical passage over the life cycle is one that involves multiple rather than single role transitions.

In part because passages are richly varied and in part because of the traditional perspectives of sociology itself, only certain types of passages and selected properties of them have been studied. According to Glaser and Strauss (1971), "sociologists have tended to assume in their analyses that status passages are fairly regularized, scheduled, and prescribed" (p. 3). As they note, this focus has tended to obscure the dynamic character of social change. Indeed, in light of our rapidly changing and highly differentiated society we already have evidence that transitions to new roles are being created. We know that institutionalized passages are undergoing criticism and revision and that the expectations and evaluations of statuses and roles are themselves being altered in the process. Minorities, youth, women, the aged, homosexuals, and students are questioning their roles in society and beginning to forge both new structures and new images of themselves. Traditional paths toward occupational success, marriage and parenthood, educational attainment, and even toward dying are being challenged. One only has to note the existence of such phenomena as decayed entry into the labor force, mid-career job changes, experimental marriages, abortion-on-demand, interrupted college careers, and seminars on dying to understand that new modes of transition are already being explored and chosen. Ideological, social, and technological changes continue to give rise to new social memberships and identities—Jesus people, feminists, single parents, acupuncturists, bisexuals, and mystics are just a few of the new structural opportunities that have already undergone initial exploration. As these and other experiments in "role making" (Turner, 1956) continue to increase in modern society, we must abandon some of our assumptions about the nature of role passages and come to terms with the emerging, fluid improvisations that mark the person-in-transit.

The aim of the present study is to explore the nature of one such passage— the transition by Roman Catholic nuns from a convent community into the secular society. We chose this particular passage from religious to secular life because of its generic character in that it involves a multiple transition of major roles and fundamental transformation of identity. It entails alterations and accommodation to the basic role sequences of lay life—aging, family, work, marriage, and friendship. These are, in turn, the social locations that shape the meanings and qualities in which our very self-images are grounded. In this light, then, it typifies the broad transformations of identities, behaviors, and social memberships that individuals experience during the life course.

The choice of this passage, beyond its generic attributes, provides a chance to investigate certain problems that are of theoretical importance but have yet to receive much systematic attention in sociology. To begin with, this passage is an *emergent* one. Glaser and Strauss (1971, pp. 85-86), who gave us the first formal theory of status passage, characterize the emergent passage as one which is created, discovered, and shaped by the parties as they go along. This contrasts with established passages which are formed by institutionalized rules, timetables, strategies, and meanings, such as marriage or education. For our purpose, we will define an emergent passage as one in which persons either create new roles or modify the institutionalized pathways of existing ones. As mentioned earlier, it is precisely this type of role passage that is seldom explored in sociological investigations and yet is increasingly significant in a society marked by continuing social improvisations.

In "emergent" passages there are, by definition, few guidelines, precedents, or models to facilitate the transfer between roles. To some extent, of course, persons can rely on general social values and expectations, previous transitions, and knowledge and skills gained from various experiences to guide their activity. Nevertheless, they are to a large degree forging new social pathways on their own. They initially may set up certain ends for themselves and begin to map out strategies for moving toward them. Periodic appraisals of the situation may occur and stock taken both of the means to reach certain goals and the goals themselves. Efforts may be made to compare problems and prospects with others involved in the same or similar transitions. As anticipated events occur or fail to materialize, priority rankings of situations or aspirations may be renegotiated. Agents of socialization may be recruited or their usefulness redefined. Intentional manipulations of personal attributes, appearance, and identities may be tried and evaluated. Standards for measuring "progress" may be erected, used, and then replaced by new ones. This type of passage, thus, is an open-ended one, full of improvisations, assessments, and modifications. It entails continuous alterations in meanings, evaluation, action, and response. As individuals breaking new ground, the persons who generate these emergent passages may experience both the heady and exciting pleasures of release, discovery, and creation as well as the uncertainty, tension, and fear that are tightly interwoven in the process of emergent social change. As Americans, we have already witnessed the emergent passages of Blacks, women, conservationists, and athletes, among others. As sociologists we are challenged to explain this phenomenon from our special perspective.

Second, the movement from nun to lay person involves a passage through *multiple* roles. In fact, only a few transitions occur which entail single or isolated transfers from one to another social location. Neither individuals nor roles are so neatly compartmentalized that we can treat them in isolation from one another. Yet, many sociological investigations of role transfers are, by necessity, handled in this manner for various analytical purposes (Kennedy & Kerber, 1972; Rossi, 1968; Smigel, 1965). By deliberately choosing to treat the passage under investigation as a multiple one we can better explore the problems of linkage (Glaser & Strauss, 1971, p. 142) between various role transfers. How do individuals rank the relative importance of each passage? How, and to what degree, does each passage affect the other? In what manner do people manage the linkages between transfers, and with what consequences for the individual and the overall sequence? This is an issue that is of special concern in a society such as ours relative to more traditional ones because, as Glaser and Strauss (1971) point out, "in industrialized societies, the burden is often on individuals to articulate their own passage" (p. 143).

To some degree, even industrialized societies provide mechanisms to facilitate the simultaneous movements of persons through age, marital, work, and other social roles. Laws, informal sanctions, values, and cultural priorities are examples of such mechanisms. They make it possible for a person to become engaged, complete college, leave the nuclear family, and continue one's unemployment without severe personal strain. Despite such mechanisms to facilitate this articulation:

> Individuals in at least the advanced sectors of industrialized societies do confront the necessity of juggling most of their own passages. This requires a host of decisions and also the creation of strategies and tactics, not to mention the choice of proper assisting agents. (Glaser & Strauss, 1971, p. 143)

Exploring the ways in which former nuns confront the simultaneous passage into and out of various roles provides an opportunity to study this nascent sociological problem.

Third, this passage is a *self-initiated* one and draws attention to the fact that individuals are active agents who make assessments of their personal and social situation and are interested in, and capable of exerting control over, various stages of their lives. More traditional conceptions of role passage in sociology have emphasized the social environment or the actor as the major sources of status and role transfers. The social actor is viewed as occupying positions, playing roles, and belonging to groups which involve him or her in reciprocal relations with others that are shaped largely by external expectations. The general expectations of these others exert demands on the individual to alter present role performances, shift group memberships, change role partners, or acquire new statuses. Their control over powerful sanctions and valued rewards, according to this view, make these others effective agents of socialization and allocation and account for much of the movement of individuals in and out of social roles. At higher levels of social organizations, the actor is viewed as belonging to a community and moving within the larger society. The processes occurring at these levels— technological innovation, population redistribution, economic and political change, legal decision, ideological shifts—filter down through the social structure and make themselves felt at the interpersonal and individual level. We can mention here jet travel, the rise of suburbia, inflation, war, desegregation laws, and the decline of the work ethic, respectively. These larger social forces thus are seen as inducements or demands for leaving certain social positions and entering others.

This conceptualization is not inaccurate; rather, it has overemphasized the external pressures for transitions by neglecting the part individuals themselves play in the process of role passage. As Clausen (1968, p. 189) has noted sociologists have not stressed the fact that actors themselves may be unsatisfied with their present roles or their performances in them and will initiate changes in one or more of these roles themselves.

When viewed in the light of increasing demands made by groups and individuals for more autonomy, along with the declining ability of our institutions to arrange, control, and predict effective modes of living, this traditional conceptualization may become less fruitful for understanding social change. In an attempt to redress this imbalance we have emphasized the self-initiated dimension of the passage from religious to secular life.[1] We conceive of the actor-in-transit as one who consciously makes choices, seeks out new roles, and experiments with alternate modes of behaving, thinking, and feeling. This conceptualization contrasts as well with the psychological view of the actor (Goslin, 1969) "as responding in more or less automatic and stable ways, as a consequence of prior experience, to configurations of stimuli coming forth from the external environment and from within the learner himself" (p. 3). We reject such a mechanical, behavioristic conception. We view the actor as one who is capable of making rational decisions and choices; who can weigh the costs of his or her actions; who possesses personal goals and needs as well as being responsive to the expectations of others; who acts to maximize his or her changes for achieving goals and continues to evaluate interpersonal and group relations; and whose orientations to the *future* are as important as "prior experience" in influencing these actions.

A fourth advantage of studying this particular passage derives from the fact that, by virtue of having been in religious life for some time period, former nuns do not move with their age-peers through the "typical" sequences of major roles over the life course. They lag behind members of their age cohort in many institutional spheres of social life—as workers, consumers, lovers, and spouses. This phenomenon has been termed *age incongruity* and *age deviance*.[2] Because expectations exist for people, at specific age levels, to have played certain roles and acquired particular skills, knowledge, and experience, these women-in-passage will face somewhat unique problems of accountability and accommodation. How does one explain and adjust to a first job, date, bank account, or apartment as a single women in her early thirties? How does one "catch-up" with age-peers in accumulating the biographical experiences associated with adulthood? What kinds of responses do others make to this age deviation and how do these responses influence successful role passage? These questions are at least implicit in

---

[1]For an example of the more traditional sociological orientation toward role change see Helen Ebaugh's (1977) *Out of the Cloister*, which stresses the structural and ideological changes in religious orders as major determinants of role passage.

[2]The concept, "age incongruity" initially was developed by Riley et al.(1972,p.413). The concept of "age deviance" is explicated in "Managing Violated Expectancies: The Age Deviant in Interaction," by Lynn Atwater—paper presented at the Annual Convention of the American Sociological Association, August, 1973.

sociological investigations of stigmatized persons who are attempting to move out of such total institutions (Goffman, 1961, pp. 4–5) as prisons, asylums, sanitaria, and orphanages. Prisoners, mental patients, orphans, and addicts confront similar problems posed by age incongruity in that they are out of synchronization with their age-peers in moving through social roles. However, the involuntary nature of their membership in total institutions and its attending stigma makes generalizations from studies of these populations highly limited.

From another perspective, focusing on the age deviance of former nuns sensitizes us to the increasing age variation of role entrance that exists in American society. Going to college, beginning a career, getting married, and raising a family are less likely than ever before to be attached to specific age expectations. This is especially true for women who, as a consequence of the feminist movement, have begun to postpone certain roles (spouse, mother volunteer) and enter others (student, worker, politician) at ages which challenge traditional expectations. In this sense, former nuns can be seen as structural pioneers who, unwittingly, were among the earliest groups to break with established connections between age and role occupancy.[3]

Lastly, as we follow women from their lives as nuns through passages to other lives our focus is kept on the *processual* nature of role occupancy. Using Glaser and Strauss' (1971) terminology, "it is important that we continue to see a status passage temporally rather than statically. Persons are in constant movement over time, not just in a status" (p. 47). Role passage will be viewed as involving three major phases or sequences—the relinquishment of one or more roles, a transitional phase of experimentation and initial accommodation, and the acquisition of new roles. In fact, detailed studies of even just one phase of an overall passage, such as parenthood, reveal that each of the three general phases may in themselves be composed of subphases (Kubler-Ross, 1969; Rossi, 1968). Failure to explore passages sequentially can lead to inadequate understanding because, as Becker (1963) cautions, "what may operate as a cause at one step in the sequence may be of negligible importance at another step" (p. 33). Thus, at each phase of the former nun's passage her problems, choices, meanings, and tactics are somewhat different than in earlier and subsequent phases. To grasp these essential differences it is necessary that we pan over the entire passage to underscore the fluidity of structural movement.

Underlying this particular study is a further specification of our model of role passage which stresses this processual theme. From a sociological perspective the relinquishment of social roles may be done voluntarily or against one's will; it may be initiated by one's self or others; it may be to some

---

[3]Hiestand (1971) suggests that the exodus of nuns in the late sixties may have served as a role model for secular women who are presently involved in alternative careers.

extent desirable or undesirable; it can be done alone or in conjunction with others; it could be inevitable or repeatable; it can vary, in other words, in terms of a host of analytical properties. These properties must be incorporated into our analysis because they will influence various aspects of relinquishment, such as one's motives for leaving a role, the kinds of preparations that are made for leave-taking, and one's assessment of the decision to abandon a certain life-style. These properties are also important because they will have an impact on the movement people make through subsequent phases of the passage as well as their eventual accommodation to new roles and ways of life.

As a number of sociologists have noted (Bredemeier & Stephenson, 1962; Riley et al., 1972), relinquishment also entails the reduction of rewards for prior behavior, expectations, values, relations, and self-conceptions. This shift in rewards involves such processes as anticipatory socialization, changes in reference groups and role models, new patterns of interaction and group membership, and personal reassessments and reconstructions of meanings and events. In addition, role-leaving entails the interplay of personal motives and actual and perceived alternatives and abilities (Brim & Wheeler, 1966, p. 25). Persons who relinquish roles voluntarily are also involved in calculations of proper timings and acceptable explanations of their decision; they may also have established certain expectations about the future and begin to develop strategies for meeting these expectations before relinquishment actually occurs.

Analytically, at least, we can separate relinquishment from the transitional phase but, as the discussion will reveal later, in actuality these separations are more difficult to delineate in strict fashion. That is, persons do not just leave a role; rather, the period of relinquishment may overlap with the next phases conceived of as "transitional statuses" (Glaser & Strauss, 1971, p. 47) in which a person moves between two or more positions. Well-known transitional phases include the honeymoon, basic training for army recruits, pregnancy, fraternity pledging, medical internships, and the like. In these transitional sequences, persons make initial accommodations to the strains and ambivalence of relinquishment. They may begin or continue to reassess the meaning of their past experience in the prior positions and its implications for their present or future behavior. They start to construct new or modified patterns of behavior, plan tactics, experiment and improvise, test, and evaluate new presentations of self.

The acquisition of new roles begins to occur in the transitional phases as persons orient themselves and their activity toward new social locations. Role acquisitions entail socialization processes that link persons with agents who identify expectations, provide facilities and resources for learning and practice, and who distribute sanctions for performance. Of special interest to us is the fact that the person moving toward emergent positions must find ways to articulate these multiple acquisitions, seek out appropriate agents, gain control over the timing and direction of these movements, handle unforeseen turns of events, and acquire validation of new role acquisitions from others.

As persons go through these phases they are also engaged in biographical reconstructions, in which past events are reinterpreted in the light of present ideas and purposes. As Berger (1963) so clearly reveals, "at least within our own consciousness, the past is malleable and flexible, constantly changing as our recollection reinterprets and reexplains what has happened" (pp. 54–55). When persons undergo rather major transitions of multiple roles and life-style, reinterpretations of biography are likely to be more conscious or deliberate and one's identity as well undergoes "transformation" (Strauss, 1959, pp. 89–109) because "a status...is likely to become a way of being as well as a way of acting." Role passages, then, entail the alteration of self-conceptions and the management of continuities in identity.

A related issue for certain passages, including the one to be discussed here, concerns the development of strategies for managing impressions, biographical information, and social and personal identities (Goffman, 1963). When persons either enter or leave social positions which are devalued or are, by virtue of affiliation with a social position, perceived as possessing undesirable attributes they are confronted with problems of "acceptance" (Goffman, 1963,p.8). The ways in which they handle these problems make up part of the process of role acquisition.

This basic sociological framework will serve as a sensitizing tool for interpreting our findings. It is also the organizing principle around which the book is shaped: Part II will focus on the relinquishment of religious roles and life-styles, Part III will contain a discussion of the initial transition to secular life, and Part IV will examine the acquisition of new roles and accommodation to new ways of living.

I have conceptualized the movement of nuns from religious to secular life as a process of passing between sets of roles and ways of life. This passage is viewed as an emergent one initiated by persons who are active participants in shaping who they are and how they live. The task before us is to allow a sociological vision to enhance our understanding of how this passage was made.

2

The Passage from Religious to Secular Life: A Case Study

The first part of this chapter contains a brief discussion of religious orders, namely, those structures and goals that form the background against which we can understand what it meant to be a member of such an order, a nun. The second part of the chapter will describe the research design employed to study the passage of nuns into the secular world.

RELIGIOUS ORDERS

Much of the mystery, confusion, and misinformation about living as a nun in a religious order has been eliminated by the appearance, over the past decade, of popular and scholarly treatments of religious life (Aronson, 1971; Cita-Malard, 1964; Griffin, 1975; Muckenhirn, 1967; Suenens, 1962). One of the best and most sociological analyses is Ebaugh's (1977) *Out of the Cloister* which offers a rich overview of the changes that have occurred in religious orders over the last twenty-five years.

Briefly, a religious order is a formal organization of either men or women which is officially recognized by the Roman Catholic Church. Members of what are termed contemplative orders are virtually isolated from contact with the outside world and devote themselves totally to prayer and meditation. Members of active orders, on the other hand, engage in a range of apostolic services or functions, such as teaching, nursing, social services, and the like. Most active orders often specialize in just one particular function and informally become known as "a teaching order," or a "missionary order."

Most religious orders of women are active ones engaged primarily in teaching. The members of religious orders are referred to either as nuns or sisters.[1]

One of the most astonishing events to occur in the history of religious orders was the large exodus of nuns leaving religious orders during the sixties. Between 1960 and 1976 the number of nuns in the U. S. dropped from approximately 168,500 to 131,000. The decline in membership began dramatically in 1967 and continued through the early seventies (Ebaugh, 1977, pp. 67–68). While this study is not concerned with explaining the sociological reasons for this significant loss of membership some background information concerning changes in religious life are important in setting the context for our study.

In 1962 Pope John XXIII initiated Vatican Council II to address itself to a reexamination of the role of the Catholic Church in modern society. One issue of concern to the council fathers was an evaluation of religious orders and, in October 1965, Vatican Council II released the document, "Decree on the Appropriate Renewal of the Religious Life" (Abbot, 1966). This document encouraged religious orders to assess their goals, policies, and structures in terms of their effectiveness in maintaining a viable religious life in contemporary society. By the end of Vatican Council II, in 1965, a challenge had gone out to all religious orders to renew themselves through critical examination and experimentation with alternate structures, roles, and relations that formed the core of religious life. While the consequences of Vatican Council II's mandate for renewal will be discussed in Chapter 3 it would be helpful for a fuller understanding of this study to describe what religious life was like prior to the Council and the subsequent efforts at renewal by religious orders.

According to Ebaugh (1977), before Vatican Council II "religious orders in the U. S. were quite homogeneous both in exterior manifestations and in the purpose and spirit that permeated them" (p. 13). The structure of authority in religious orders was clearly defined and strictly hierarchical in nature. Members of an order elected a group of representatives, known as the "general chapter," which served as the major governing group in the order. These representatives elected a mother general who, as the highest official in the order, wielded considerable authority in the administration of the order. The mother general, in addition to her other functions, "had the power to assign sisters to the jobs they were to perform, to decide where and with whom they were to live, what daily schedule they were to follow, and who was to be

---

[1]Officially, the terms "congregation" and "order" as well as "sister" and "nun" refer to differences in the structure and function of religious organizations and to the type of vows taken by members of the collectivity. For our purposes, these terms will be used interchangeably as is accepted in common lay usage.

the local superior in each house in which sisters resided" (Ebaugh, 1977, p. 19).

The life of a nun in these orders was highly prescribed and routinized. Formal and informal mechanisms of control were elaborated to govern the nuns' thoughts, beliefs, and behavior. Enforced isolation from the outside world and rigorous resocialization[2] within the religious community served to generate the radical change in identity, commitment, and behavior required to be a nun.

The making of a nun was the result of careful and extended resocialization that took place over three distinct stages. At each stage the young woman was encouraged to give up her prior self-image, commitments, and world view and learn to find rewarding those demanded by her new role as a nun. The postulancy was the first stage of this preparation and lasted generally for one year. As a postulant, the young woman was given a black uniform, stripped of her personal possessions, strictly limited to infrequent contact with family and friends, and segregated with other postulants who collectively began to learn the general expectations of being a nun.

If she successfully completed this initial period the postulant proceeded to the next stage—the novitiate. The novitiate year was one of total isolation from anyone except other novices. In a rich, ceremonial rite of passage novices received the habit or dress of a nun, a religious name, and a new identity as "brides of Christ." This year was one dedicated to prayer, introspection, and preparation for formal entrance into the order.

The final stage in becoming a nun was termed professed religious life. If she was officially accepted by the mother general and the council, the nun took vows of poverty, chastity, and obedience which were renewed annually for a specified number of years (ranging from three to six years depending on the order). During these years the nun continued to be closely supervised. Her access to the outside world, through personal contact, exposure to the mass media, and physical mobility was highly regulated. Her vows required the renunciation of material goods and services, the abandonment of all sexual activity, and the willing and complete submission to the authority of her superiors. If her dedication to this way of life was personally acceptable to her and to her superiors, she then made a permanent commitment to religious life and took final or perpetual vows which bound her for life to her community. Only for grave reasons was a nun able to receive a dispensation from final vows and this permission had to be granted from Rome.

To be a nun, then, prior to Vatican Council II, was to live in a total institution that demanded complete uniformity of thought, belief, and action.

---

[2]Resocialization is a concept which refers to socialization that involved a radical departure from prior identity and experience to produce dramatic differences in self-image, beliefs, and behavior.

A nun had to abandon her prior identity and way of life and willingly take on new modes of being and living. Part of this population of nuns, those who ultimately decided to abandon religious life, forms the subject matter of this study. Before we examine the impact on the life-style of nuns resulting from the renewal efforts by religious orders, I want to present a description of how the research for this study was conducted.

METHODOLOGY

Both theoretically and substantively the passage from religious to secular life is a relatively uncharted sociological area.[3] As such, it shaped the objectives of the study and the way the research was designed. Basically, the aim of this work was exploration rather than hypothesis testing.[4] That is, given the minimal amount of exploratory work done in this area the study was designed with the intention of generating insights, sensitizing concepts, and hypotheses about this type of role passage. While the testing of hypotheses is important in sociological theorizing," . . . it is often difficult to formulate good hypotheses until a considerable amount of exploratory work has been carried out. Premature preoccupation with specific hypotheses may divert attention from the broad exploration of social systems in the round" (Riley, 1963, p. 15).

Utilizing a general sociological model of role passage, which is explicited at various points throughout the book, and having chosen exploration as the basic objective, the research design began to take shape.[5] Since I was interested in how individuals passed from one set of roles to another, the design called for the research case to be the individual-in-a-role. Given the exploratory nature of the research I chose to study intensively a small number of cases (twenty former nuns) in order to concentrate in depth and detail on the complexities of the particular passage under investigation. The unique advantage of the case study is its ability to provide access to a wide range of data and to uncover latent patterns of behavior of which respondents themselves may not be fully aware. In the case of former nuns, these advantages are crucial for an understanding of the multiple emergent passage through which they passed. Naturally, case studies involving small numbers limit the generality of findings but if they are chosen carefully and analyzed systematically they can yield rich insights that provide the basis for detailed

---

[3]In addition to Ebaugh's (1977) study, see a popular treatment such as Monica Baldwin's *I Leap Over the Wall,* (1950) for a scholarly work see Molitor (1967).

[4]See Riley (1963, pp. 14–15) for a discussion of these two different research objectives.

[5]See Riley (1963, pp. 16–25) for a detailed description of the alternaive decisions that are involved in designing a piece of research.

testing on larger samples.[6] Since other aspects of the research design require more detailed discussion, they will be treated as special subsections.

The Research Instrument

The data for this study were collected through the use of the intensive interview. I was interested in discovering the respondents' meanings, attitudes, sentiments, and experiences that formed and directed their movement through a major role passage. As Riley (1963) points out, responses to questions, "although they do not always report interaction as the observer might perceive it, have the peculiar merit of reflecting directly the subjective states of the actor, the underlying disposition to act" (p. 167). Also, she notes:

> Questioning reveals the structure of orientations—the subjective patterns of attitudes, feelings, mutual expectations, and interpersonal relationships among the members—that underlie the overt interaction, but are not always accessible to observation. (p. 167)

The selection of the interview technique was made, then, to capture the subjectively experienced interplay between the personal and structural factors involved in such passages. I wanted to get as full a picture as possible of what it meant to have left religious life, how a nun became a lay person, what emotions and relations were activated during the passage, and how she accommodated herself to the dilemmas, enticements, and changes in herself and her ties to others.

The interview instrument itself (a copy of the interview guide can be found in the Appendix) was a composite of three types of interviews, each chosen for its particular advantages in questioning respondents. One part of the interview was structured to collect the same information from all respondents through the same wording of questions for all respondents. Objective pieces of data, which respondents could easily answer, were obtained through this schedule of questions which included such information as the respondent's length of time in religious life, educational level at the time of exit, and marital status at time of interview. The second form used in the interview is known as the nonschedule standardized interview (Richardson et al., 1965). Here, the same *classes* of information were obtained from each respondent but the types of questions used to derive the information were not the same. The use of this type of interview is based on the assumption that a fixed sequence of

---

[6]There are detailed discussions of the relative merits of case studies in virtually all social science methodology texts. The important issue, in finally deciding on the number of cases to be studied, is the appropriate match between the researcher's objectives and the nature of the subject matter itself.

the same questions fails to do justice to the fact that questions must be formulated in ways and in sequences that respondents find meaningful and to which they can respond (Richardson et al., 1965, pp. 46–49). The flexibility of this form of interview, in terms of both the phrasing and sequence of questions, also has the advantage of being especially useful in dealing with sensitive topics or topics about which the respondent lacks a clear or stable formulation. This type of interview was useful, for example, in questioning the respondent's decision to leave religious life or how she resumed social and dating roles after leaving the convent. A third part of the interview was nonstandardized, which allows the interviewer to discover insights or unanticipated areas developing in the course of an interview and to follow up on them with the respondent. This strategy is especially important in exploratory research since the unexpected or latent finding is able to emerge through its use. To give but one example, I pursued with a few respondents their account of how they consciously engaged in invidious competition with other nuns in terms of physical attractiveness by manipulating their habit and other articles of wear. This finding, in turn, suggested to me a possible link between covert anticipatory socialization and the subsequent adjustment to sex-role demands.

The final version of the interview instrument was a product of two sets of activities. For four years prior to carrying out this study I was on the faculty at a Catholic university which gave me the opportunity to observe, speak, and interact with hundreds of women who were at varying stages in the process of withdrawal from religious life. Without knowing until a few years later that I would be carrying out research in this area I was able to gather a personal and sociological familiarity with some basic themes surrounding this passage. Once I had decided to study this topic I conducted pilot interviews with eight former nuns during the winter of 1971–1972. These interviews were carried out with women from different types of religious orders (varying in terms of the order's size, its geographical location, ethnic composition, and primary function); each respondent was interviewed on two or three occasions, with each interview lasting three to four hours. None of these respondents was included in the final sample for the study, as is usually the case in pilot studies.

The Sample

In selecting a sample, the researcher is always guided by the way in which a problem is conceptualized and the objectives of the research process itself. Of the many ways to study the phenomena occurring in religious orders during the last decade I chose to focus on the emergent, self-initiated, multiple passage of nuns from one set of roles and life-styles to others. The objective was to explore, in considerable detail, how this passage was created by analyzing certain social processes and arrangements. Guided by the general conceptualization of this type of passage and the more specific insights gained from the pilot interviews my aim in selecting a sample was twofold. First, I wanted to select a small number of cases that could be studied intensively and second, I wanted to choose the sample in such a way that it would facilitate the analysis of certain variables which seemed important to this type of passage. While much sociological research is designed for a representational sample in order to generalize the findings, other studies, such as this one, place more emphasis on sampling for the purpose of analysis, especially when the research is exploratory (Riley 1963, pp. 282–283, 295–304). Nevertheless, as discussed below, a number of steps were taken to make the sample approximate some of the more typical dimensions of religious life in the U.S.

In selecting the sample for the study my goal was to try to control for a number of extraneous variables that would enable me to concentrate on the variables of interest in the research—the explanatory variables (Riley, 1963, p. 298).

The first sampling decision, then, was to select all respondents from the same religious order, thus providing a common organizational context for all respondents which minimized the different impact of organizational variables on the carrying out of the passage. The next decision concerned which order to select from the approximately 400 religious orders in the U.S.[7] Religious orders vary in many ways, some of the more important differences being their geographical location, size of membership, duration of the order, location of the motherhouse within or outside the U.S., the ethnic composition of members, and the primary function of the order. Equally important for the present study, orders varied according to the degree of change occurring in the order as a result of the Vatican II call for renewal. While I had no way of knowing at the time of selecting the sample how these factors might influence the nuns' passage to secular life (nor was this my primary research concern) my aim was to select a religious order that would hold constant some of these organizational variables. I wanted to select an order that would not be unique in terms of the majority of religious orders in the U. S. and thus used the following criteria for selection of the order: (1) the motherhouse of the order, the major administrative unit, was located in the U. S.; (2) the major function of the order was teaching; (3) the membership was at least 100 nuns; (4) the membership was not predominantly drawn from a well-defined, cohesive ethnic or national group; (5) the order had a geographical location within range of a major metropolitan area of the U. S.; and (6) a moderate amount of change (as determined by judgments made by nuns and former nuns to which I had access) had occurred in the order's structure of religious life. While any further specification might jeopardize the anonymity of the chosen order, I

---

[7]The Official Catholic Directory is the only public source of data containing statistical information on the religious orders in the U.S. For a discussion of the limitations of such data, see Ebaugh (1977, p. 142).

felt that these six bases of selection fairly approximate the general profile of a religious order in the U.S.[8]

With these criteria in mind the next step was to select one particular order that satisfied the above criteria and to which I could gain entrée. The difficulty of gaining access to religious orders is well known to social science researchers and discussed openly by Ebaugh (1977, p. xiii), herself a former nun and present sociologist. I was no exception. Written inquiries and personal interviews with the religious superiors of seven orders that met the selection criteria failed to produce the maximum cooperation needed—obtaining a sampling frame of all the members who had voluntarily left the religious order from 1965 (the final year of Vatican Council II) to 1972 (the year the research was carried out). Finding official access blocked,[9] I decided to rely on informal sources—particularly nuns and former nuns of these orders who agreed to compile as complete a list as possible of the names and addresses of former nuns from their orders. I finally chose the one order which met all the criteria for selection and for which I had obtained the most complete sampling frame. Two interesting observations are relevant here. To some extent a full list of all potential respondents was impossible because some former nuns had married and therefore could not be located through their unknown married names. This inability to "find" women who fail to keep their maiden names remains a latent cost to researchers of sexist social designations. On the other hand, a fortuitous consequence of the continuation of relations between former nuns who had left religious life, along with occasional "reunions" they held over the years, was a more complete list than I would have otherwise obtained.

A list of the names and addresses of 63 former nuns who left the order between 1965 and 1972 was thus compiled and, with the help of nuns and former nuns from this order, it was possible to obtain general information about each respondent on the basis of which they would be selected for the interview. As stated earlier, this sample of former nuns was not intended to be representative of the population of all former nuns. Rather, it was selected with the purpose of being able to explore, as a case study, the transaction from religious to secular life. The variables used to select the sample were suspected of having significance in influencing different aspects of the passage. They should serve to differentiate respondents from one another in such a way as to

---

[8]Ebaugh's (1977) data on religious orders, while not available at the time of the present research, lends support to the general usefulness of having chosen these criteria for selecting the order to be studied.

[9]Letters were written to the National Association of Women Religious and the Conference of Major Superiors of Women requesting information on religious orders. The former organization merely referred me to the Official Catholic Directory, the latter organization failed to respond even to follow-up requests. The Chancery Office (the administrative arm of a diocese) was also appealed to but I was told no records were kept on the amount of membership loss in religious orders. These and other abortive attempts underscore some of the continuing resistance to social science research in selected areas of social life.

permit the emergence of variations in the ways in which the passage was experienced and managed by the respondents. On the basis of my informal discussions with former nuns and the pilot interviews I had conducted, the following factors appeared to be analytically important in selecting the sample: the number of years spent in religious life; age at time of leaving; type of vow taken before leaving; length of time in secular life; occupation and marital status at the time of sample selection. After stratifying the respondents according to these variables a judgment sample (Riley, 1963, p. 302) was used to select twenty-one respondents to be interviewed.[10] By preselecting the respondents I hoped to avoid the many biases entailed in the self-selection of research cases. Personal contact was then made with each of the respondents to discuss the nature of the research and to solicit her cooperation; only one respondent refused to cooperate and the final sample consisted of twenty former nuns. The profile of the twenty respondents who agreed to participate is characterized as follows:

1. Number of Years Spent in Religious Life:
   5 to 7 years .... 4 (respondents)
   8 to 14 years 10
   15 years or more 6
2. Type of Vows Taken at Time of Leaving Religious Life:
   Final vows 16
   Temporary vows 4
3. Age of Respondent at Time of Leaving Religious Life:
   25–29 3
   30–34 9
   35–39 5
   40 or over 3
4. Number of Years in Secular Life at Time of Interview:
   Less than 1 year 2
   1 to 2 years 4
   2 to 3 years 7
   3 to 4 years 4
   Over 4 years 3
5. Marital Status at Time of Interview:
   Single 14
   Married or Engaged 6
6. Occupation Held at Time of Interview:
   Academic (teaching, counseling) 10
   Nonacademic 7
   Not employed 3

---

[10]By using a judgment rather than probability sample I hoped to decrease chance error, which increases with a small sample size. Although more accurate statistics regarding the profile of nuns who left religious orders in the last decade have recently become available (Ebaugh, 1977), at the time of this study informal estimates had indicated that the largest category of nuns who were leaving were in their late twenties and thirties, were close to or had taken final vows, and that the peak years of leaving were between 1967 and 1969 (Neal, 1968; Papa, 1971). Ebaugh's data generally supports these initial estimates. I had, then, some knowledge of the significant profile of the respondents and tried to choose a sample that best approximated it.

Even though the aim of this research was exploratory I did hope that the experiences of my sample of twenty former nuns would be personally recognizable to some wider population of women who had left religious life. The particular order from which I drew my sample was one way in which I attempted to increase the generality of my findings. In addition, while I was collecting the data for this research I also did in-depth interviews with seven former nuns who had left religious orders that differed in size, ethnic composition, primary apostolic function, and degree of organizational change from the order I had chosen. Many of the findings from these interviews were not substantially different from the data I had collected from my sample. While certain differences did emerge that could be related to variations in the types of orders, the similarities of basic themes in the two sets of interviews gave me confidence that the experiences reported by my sample respondents were not primarily a function of variations in organizational characteristics.

Data Collection

The interviews were conducted during the spring and summer of 1972. Each interview was taped and lasted approximately four hours. In a few instances the complexity of the material required that some respondents be interviewed on two occasions. The interviews were carried out either in the home of the respondent, the home of the researcher, or the researcher's university office, the choice being dictated by the feasibility and privacy afforded by each location.

As participants in sociological research the respondents were quite ideal from a researcher's point of view. They were highly eager to participate in the study and personally concerned about the issues raised in the research. They had obviously given considerable thought to the topic under investigation and were willing to talk about their experiences in a candid manner. As intelligent, introspective, and articulate women they helped to facilitate a complex interview process. Indeed, many of them expressed intellectual as well as personal interest in the problem of how persons leave one way of life for another. Given these circumstances rapport was rather easy to generate and sustain in most of the interviews. I also suspect that, for many of them, the interviews served some cathartic function. At different points in the interview respondents indicated that they had not discussed a certain event or sentiment with even their closest friend, relative, or spouse and expressed relief at having had a chance to express themselves on the subject. It was often at these points that the interview process became taxing for both participants. To recall and reexperience the pain, anger, fear, and guilt involved in some parts of the passage presented a strong, albeit different, emotional challenge to both of us.[11] All the respondents indicated that they had enjoyed the chance to share their experiences and had profited in some way by the interview. Some were more ambivalent, however, and noted that they did not welcome the reawakening of some unpleasant memories of their passage to secular life. In fact, the only member of the sample who refused to be interviewed indicated this possibility as her reason for refusing to be involved in the research.

The only strong concern expressed by all respondents dealt with the matter of confidentiality of material and personal anonymity. They were quite aware of the public curiosity, mystery, and myth surrounding their personal lives and requested complete confidentiality from me in exchange for their candor. Each respondent was assured that all interview material would be kept in strict confidence and that I would alter all information that could identify their order and any other material that would be personally revealing. I have attempted to be faithful to this promise without jeopardizing the accuracy of the findings.

Finally, personal reflection on the research process had led me to believe that my own Roman Catholic background helped to facilitate the design and implementation of this research. Although I was never a nun I was brought up in the subculture of Roman Catholicism and intimately exposed to its values, rituals, jargon, myths, and meanings. My familiarity with parts of the lives of nuns helped me in two ways as a sociological researcher. First, I could make more efficient use of the time needed for interviewing because I did not have to ask certain questions, such as What is a Motherhouse? What is the novitiate? Second, my familiarity with religious life gave the respondent a sense of being able to communicate with someone who had some understanding of the skeletal structure of her situation. In this sense, it helped to enhance rapport and confidence in the interview. Naturally, I had to be careful not to assume that I knew the *meanings* a respondent gave to certain statements nor to suggest to her that she could make such an assumption. For example, although I knew the official definition of perpetual or final vows I would ask the respondent to explain how she interpreted the taking of these vows and what they meant to her at different stages in her religious life.

The analysis that follows will be qualitative in nature and consist of a blending of two themes—one intellectual, the other experiential. All research and subsequent interpretation is guided by ideas and theories about the subject matter under investigation. A conceptual model—consisting of these theoretical ideas—serves as a map of the territory to be explored and an organizing image of the phenomenon being investigated. As an intellectual

---

[11]In light of these experiences as an interviewer in an emotionally charged area I would support the idea of incorporating more psychologically oriented skills in the training of sociologists for use of the depth interview.

endeavor, the questions raised and the interpretation offered about this passage have been shaped by the particular model or sociological framework offered in skeletal fashion in Chapter 1. In the chapters that follow we will test the adequacy of the model because this is, essentially, the goal of all research. As Riley (1963) notes, we are obliged as scholars "... to supplement or test the ideas with which the research began—to extend, revise, specify, confirm, or discard the conceptual model" (p. 7).

On the pages that follow, however, are also the experiences, meanings, and perceptions of people who, like all of us, are participants in the drama of social life. I have attempted, through extensive quotations from the respondents, to capture their subjectively experienced passage so that we can recognize them not merely as subjects of sociological research but as individual explorers of our social terrain.

PART II
THE PROCESS OF RELINQUISHMENT

3

Making the Decision to Leave

When persons have decided to relinquish a way of life and to withdraw from major roles, we often find ourselves asking questions about motives. Why did they make that decision? What motivated that choice? Behind these concerns about motives, however, we soon find a complex array of other issues that force our attention beyond individual motivation. Many other personal attributes and social forces must be pieced together if we are to fully appreciate the rich cloth out of which is woven a decision to leave a major social role.

As we mentioned earlier, the decade of the sixties was a time of crisis and change in the Roman Catholic Church and in religious orders (Kavanagh, 1967; Westhues, 1968) which forms the background against which our discussion unfolds. Of special interest to us were the challenges and innovations taking place in hundreds of convents across the country. Nuns were questioning the authority of superiors and the hierarchical structures of religious communities. New forms of service to lay people were being suggested. The meaning of religious life and its relation to the secular society were under review. New modes of dress, new relationships, and new living arrangements were tried out. These, and a host of other improvisations in religious life were generated and sustained from two sources. One, as I have already indicated, came from within the Roman Catholic Church itself. Vatican Council II, the writings and lectures of theologians and religious leaders such as Cardinal Suenens' *The Nun in the World* (1962), and the grass roots activities of priests and nuns all came together to dramatically change the structure of religious life and the role of the nun in the modern world. A second source of change came from the larger society itself. The sixties was a decade of movement away from authority, hierarchy, regulation, and rationality. Criticism of conventional morality, traditional life-styles, modes of interpersonal relations, and the distribution of power between groups gave rise to a variety of social movements that lent ideological support to the efforts at renewal within religious life. Let us move now to look more closely at how nuns experienced these times and the impact these changes had on their coming to leave religious life.

CONDITIONS FOR RELINQUISHMENT

The decision to leave the convent was a decision to leave a way of life to which one had once been committed. Being a nun was a vocation or calling to a life very different from that of most other people. It entailed rigorous training, demanded total involvement, and exerted a profound influence on identity. Thus, the decision would involve cutting oneself off from experiences, routines, relations, and self-images that were valued and comfortable while, at the same time, exposing the individual to roles, meanings, situations, and relationships for which she was not accustomed or did not completely embrace. Like any other major decision, this one was a consequence of both individual and social forces interacting with one another.

The order from which our respondents left was, like many others, engaged in the task of renewal and experimentation. The nuns, in both formal "renewal chapters" and informal gatherings, debated the viability of their order's present form of government, its constitution and general philosophy of religious life, and the routine structures that governed job assignments, residence, communication, prayer, and dress codes. During a span of three years, from 1966 to 1969, the order experimented with alternate rules, structures, and philosophies. While this order was more open to change than some, it was not changing as rapidly as others.[1] At the time the data were collected the order had reduced its hierarchical structure of authority to allow for more involvement by members in the goverance of the community. Nuns had greater choice in the types of jobs and tasks they were to perform. They were permitted to experiment with different modes of dress. They had some choice in where and with whom they would live. They were given more freedom to associate with outsiders and to entertain family and friends. They had greater discretion in how they spent their money and used their leisure time. In many ways their lives as nuns were changing from what they had been prior to Vatican Council II. This is not to say, however, that there was consensus and equanimity in the process of bringing about these changes. Debates between groups of nuns were often bitter and frustrating; priorities were hotly contested and opposition clearly expressed. Sides were drawn and

---

[1]See Ebaugh (1977, pp.60–62) for a discussion of the range of structural change exhibited in religious orders during the post-Vatican II renewal period.

redrawn as a variety of issues came up for critical review. Temporary consensus would often dissipate as new ideas and suggestions were brought up for examination. It was, in general, a time of turmoil, hope, disappointment, fear, and promise.

Motivation to Leave Religious Life

Our respondents played different parts in this unfolding drama which leads us to look at the first step in their decision to leave religious life—the desire or motivation to relinquish the role of a nun. We have classified their primary motivation for leaving, as it was expressed by the respondents, into two categories. The first refers to the nun's evaluation of the changes that were occurring in her order as either being too extreme or too conservative for her vision of what religious life should be. This motive can be viewed as *ideological* in nature since it entails an assessment of the changes in religious life in terms of a set of interests and values grounded in a vested vision of what religious communities should be. Let us look first at those former nuns who felt that the changes were not far-reaching enough for them.

These respondents, inclined toward intellectual and introspective evaluation, were in the forefront of the demand for social change. They were in their late twenties and early thirties, had taken final vows, were active in community affairs, and either going to graduate school or participating in religious and secular institutes, workshops, and councils. Labeled "radicals" by the more conservative nuns within the order, they were asking for dramatic changes in the conventional forms of religious life. At first, their aim was to reform convent life, not to leave it. However, after experiencing repeated resistance to their proposals for change, they began to consider whether or not they could remain in a way of life that they found lacking in many respects. As one respondent puts it:

> Until about seven or eight years ago I just automatically functioned without too much thought—I guess due to training—and I started to think, not about leaving but just about convent life and my role in it. I started to think for myself, form my own opinions. I think a big influence at that time was Cardinal Suenens' *The Nun in the World.* I remember reading that and thinking, "Ah, hah! He agrees with me." Then we started having meetings at the Motherhouse discussing what was going to happen in our community. I talked a lot to people who both agreed and disagreed with me and we finally began to confront Mother and the Council with demands for significant change, as I've told you. We met with resistance at almost every turn; only token changes were permitted, and I began to wonder whether or not I could and should stay in. If I felt that the community was one that I could have lived in with my ideas and that there would not be conflict, I probably would not have thought about leaving; but I began to feel that change was not going to come about within the community. We would vote on things but the authorities would do it their way anyway . . . I began to realize then that change wasn't going to come, and to think about what I was going to do in response to this.

For this type of nun the primary motive for leaving was the slow pace of religious change. She still believed in the value of religious life but despaired over the possibility of religious roles and convent structures ever changing enough to meet her expectations and values. As another put it:

> I feel like I had a vocation and wasn't permitted to keep it because the community would not change nor make a place for us in it. I feel cheated in some way. I wanted to do this (live in a religious community)—why couldn't it have been?

Other respondents found the changes that did take place unsettling. Their security and sense of meaning as nuns were closely tied to traditional religious roles, routines, and behaviors. When these underwent challenge and revision, it undermined their commitment to religious life. Two former nuns poignantly stress this dilemma[2]:

> With all these changes in the convent I didn't see religious living a life any different from the families and people with whom you worked everyday. The sense of community was gone. I think you could say that we lived in a community just because there was a group of people living in the same house. As time passed and people went on their own, there was nothing special about this group. I think this is what really caused me to think seriously about wanting to leave.
>
> * * * * * *
>
> The liberals went too far to the left with the freedom thing. It turned me off and may have been the deciding factor in my leaving because I felt there was no element of community. I could be doing the same thing at home that I'm doing there for all anybody cares. I couldn't be one of these one-foot-in-one-foot-out religious. (What do you mean by that?) Many of them were doing things socially and emotionally that I felt were not legitimate. They called themselves religious, but they were doing many things that other lay women do. So, there was no room for me in the community. I wasn't for going back to the old days of rigid authoritarian life, but the changes were going to another extreme now and I didn't fit anywhere.

Thus, the *same* degree of change within a given order was perceived and evaluated differently by different nuns. Some felt the changes had gone too far while others viewed them as not substantial enough to retain their commitment to religious life.

The second motive for leaving was more *personal* in nature and centered around the goodness of fit that was perceived to exist between the demands of the religious role and one's personal desires and aspirations. These evaluations were also made in light of the changes occurring within the order

---

[2]Henceforth, asterisks between quoted material indicates commentary from a different respondent. No respondents are consistently identified by a case number or name in order to assure their anonymity.

but the issue for these nuns was not a concern over the most effective structures and goals for religious life. Rather, it was over whether or not the religious role itself fit well with one's personality attributes, individual needs, and ambitions:

> We were talking at that time about what "community" really meant and people were writing about meaningful relations with people, open relations, and gradually I began to realize that I needed the closer community with just one other—a romantic relationship and marriage. I couldn't have that as a nun, but this is what I found I wanted. For others it wasn't an issue. For me, it became "the" issue.
>
> * * * * * *
>
> It's not that I think being a nun is useless. For some people it's fine, but for me, no. I came to realize as the changes were going on, that I wanted to be free, that I liked to make all my choices, that the religious role wasn't "me" but something I had to force myself into.

While these respondents could see the religious role as valid for certain people, another respondent rejected it as implausible for everyone.

> Being a nun had no meaning for me at all—it was an unnatural existence. And not only for me. I don't see how anybody could live the kind of life it requires. I don't believe in it for anyone. That's how far I had come in my thinking.

For these respondents, the changes in religious life activated different kinds of questions, more intimate individualized ones that centered on self-fulfillment, happiness, and personal autonomy.

In looking at motivation, then, we find two primary themes. Nuns in the first category were ideologically motivated and can be viewed as having been "pushed" out of religious life as a consequence of changes taking place in their order. As a number of respondents in this group in fact described their leave-taking as being "more of a push than a pull." Those, however, who came to view the role of a nun as restrictive of personal inclinations, attributes, and aspirations were "pulled" or attracted by options and alternatives unavailable to them as long as they remained nuns. These differences of "push or pull" are obviously ones of degree but, as we will show later, they have consequences for the subsequent shape and accommodation that respondents make to the overall transition. What should be underscored here, however, are two observations. As sociological wisdom suggests, one's commitment to a role does depend on what occurs in the surrounding social environment. The changes that took place in religious orders did, indeed, have a variety of consequences for a nun's commitment to her role. Thus we can state that changes in the social system in which a role is embedded can generate conditions that may lead to relinquishment. As Glaser and Strauss (1971) note, "structural conditions (both contextual and situational) can render a passage reversible" (p. 21) and we have already observed the impact of changes in the structure of religious life on a nun's desire to remain in the convent.

However, we should be careful not to attribute too much influence solely to structural changes. People do not respond uniformly and automatically to changes in their social environment nor do their roles have the same meaning for each of them. As reflective social beings, persons bring to their roles and milieu different perceptions, priorities, and emphases that produce variation in their response to structural change. Even when persons share common structural locations they do not necessarily respond in similar ways. For example, approximately one-half of our sample left for ideological reasons, the other half for personal ones. However, when we compared nuns in terms of their number of years in religious life, type of vow taken, educational level, or age at which they left the convent we did not find close relations between their motives to leave and these structural variables. The one exception, mentioned earlier, was the so-called "radical nun" who felt the changes were too meager to keep her in religious life. We could speculate on the endless range of social and psychological factors that shape motivation. However, this is not our intent. What we found is that, holding constant the degree and kind of structural change in a given order, members had different responses— some were motivated to remain in the convent while others wanted to leave and did so for different reasons. Does this mean that the degree of structural change in religious orders has no bearing on motivation? It does not. Ebaugh's (1977, pp. 105–114) research shows a significant relation between the degree of change in a religious order and the primary motivation for a nun's decision to leave religious life. She found that nuns left liberal and conservative orders for reasons related to structural changes in the church and within their orders while nuns left moderate-change orders for primarily personal reasons. While this finding underscores the impact of external changes in structures our findings highlight the more personalized responses people make to the same structural changes. It is this more personalized response that we wish to underscore here, without undermining the significance of an emphasis on social structures. Each set of findings reflects a truthful, albeit different, vision of social reality.

According to our model, role relinquishment is a process that entails not just motives but knowledge of alternatives and perceptions of abilities (see Brim and Wheeler 1966, p. 25). It is not enough to *want* to leave a role or way of life. Persons must also be *aware* of alternative structural opportunities as well as come to define themselves as *able* to make use of these opportunities. Indeed, the interview data reveal that these three conditions—motivation, knowledge of alternatives, and perceptions of abilities—appear in approximately this order as the process of relinquishment unravels itself. In addition, as we shall see later, each of these conditions interacts with the other two, feeding back into and affecting them. The search for alternative roles and life-styles by nuns who began to question their desire to remain in the convent will now be examined.

The Search for Alternatives

Once a nun began to seriously entertain the thought of leaving, she was likely to pose other types of questions:

> (When you say that wanting to leave was "just a part of getting out" what do you feel were the other parts to it, so to speak?)
> Well, as I was thinking about wanting to leave I began to ask, "What would I do if I left?" "What would I be?" "Where could I go?" I wondered if the alternatives to religious life would be good for me. What were they? Would I like them?

The mass media, as we know, has become the major source of information about ideas, occupations, life-styles, and our world in general. The increasing freedom of access to the media given to nuns by their order helped to make them more aware of alternative options for implementing their values, beliefs, and needs in secular society. As one respondent observes:

> We read papers, watched TV and the news, went to movies—not like the old days when these were forbidden—and so we knew that other people and groups were doing some of the things we wanted to do, like inner-city work, communal living, changing institutions.

On a more interpersonal level, as well, nuns began to take advantage of their enlarged opportunities to become more involved in the secular society. Certain convents encouraged greater contact with the local community; some nuns went to graduate school; others joined local programs and institutes. These nuns began to encounter new types of people, occupations, ideas, relationships, and experiences that expanded their awareness of alternatives to religious life. One respondent reflects on her experiences in new social groups:

> We worked with an encounter group and . . . a teacher training program and through both of those we just met all kinds of people, all different types. (You said that these experiences began to change your thinking?) Up until that time I got involved, I was still fighting the community and debating if I should stay or leave. After I began to see that there were all these other people on the outside who were more in tune with the way I thought, I decided I wasn't going to fight the community anymore . . . I guess that the community started to become less and less important to me as I found other groups and people I could be involved with.

Another former nun comments on the impact of going to graduate school:

> I was in graduate school in the summer and meeting new people with exciting ideas, doing different kinds of things, having new ideas, and I thought that I could see myself like some of them.

Two respondents recall the consequences of participating in religious groups:

> That year I was in Bay City we had the religious education program and I became close to men; they were priests, but they were men and we called them by their first name. It was the first time I had called a man by his first name since I went in—of course, besides men in my family. So, it began to be attractive to me. (What did?) The idea . . . I think friendships with men, more than even marriage at that point. Before, we didn't have the opportunity to even have male friends!
> * * * * * *
> Making the Cursillo (a religious encounter-group experience) really affected me deeply. Before that I had been concerned with externals—rules and things—but after the Cursillo I realized there was a whole new dimension to me as a person. I could feel, be open, respond genuinely to others—things I thought were not a part of me before.

The effect of even informal encounters, a matter carefully regulated before Vatican Council II, is noted by a respondent:

> Our convent was far away from the Motherhouse and we had a lot of freedom and during those two years I began to go out and meet people in the area and began to have a great deal more confidence built up in me—more than I ever had before. I began to realize that there are other things I can do, that people liked me, that I could be of help.

This increasing awareness of alternatives experienced directly by some nuns was shared indirectly by others. Nuns one respected, those one worked with, one's close friends began to bring to the convent these new experiences, priorities, and challenges to convent life. They were the topic of conversation and debate at the supper table, in the community room, in the car, and in the faculty rooms. In this way, knowledge of options was shared, accumulated, and cultivated by nuns, each bringing some piece of the lay world to the others for their consideration.

Thus, as these women became increasingly aware of alternatives, they incorporated this knowledge into assessments of their present situation and in many cases this knowledge worked to enhance their motivation to leave. In learning about or being exposed to alternatives, the nun came to compare her life with what she knew was available to her in the secular world:

> The more exposure I had to being outside and the more I began to make my own decisions the more the (convent) rules began to bother me. We were permitted to associate more closely with lay people and I began to fit into that and enjoy it. Once I was exposed to adult living I wasn't sure that mature people could live that kind of structured religious life.
> * * * * * *
> During the summer school sessions we had a chance to attend a conference where a priest said that male–female relationships were very, very important in the development of the person and you shouldn't deny yourself these things. The people down there were beginning to act on that kind of message. Someone of

the opposite sex would be in class and you'd say go for a coke and say to yourself, "This is good. This is something I should have—a male/female relationship." I felt this was good and had a few platonic friendships myself and I enjoyed them, and with the enjoyment of all that I began to say, "Maybe this is for me."

As these comparisons were made, some nuns began to define their newly found options as more attractive than the alternatives available to them as nuns. For some, the costs of remaining as nuns loomed larger than the rewards for remaining in religious life.

Perceived Abilities

The third condition of role relinquishment centers on coming to define oneself as *able* to assume the alternative roles and life-styles of which one had become aware. This stage overlaps with the prior one in the sense that being exposed to alternatives, especially at the interactional level, provides the nun with a chance to gauge or test her own abilities because coming to see oneself as able to play other roles depends, in part, on receiving feedback from others that signals a degree of competence. For the nuns contemplating a move to secular life, they must believe that they can function in the secular world— that they can get a job, find a place to live, date and marry, make new friends, and be able to cope with all sorts of changes. A nun describes the situation poignantly:

> From the time I had thought that maybe I would be leaving I was very conscious, when I was outside, of looking at people and thinking to myself, "Do I want to be one of them?" I think the whole idea was that in the convent I knew what the rest of my life would be—but I'd look at each person—I'd look at old people very, very much—just looking at them. Or just seeing big crowds, which I had been in for all these years, you know, but never really took notice of. I was, like, with them, but I never really had to concern myself with keeping up with them and now I kept thinking, "Can I do it?" "Will I make it?"

The interviews reveal that the nun goes through a process of "sounding out" the environment, searching for confirmations of her ability to succeed outside religious life. In the passages quoted above, we see how some nuns were already beginning to develop a sense of competence in meeting new people, making friends with men, employing different skills, and the like.

As we will discuss later, all but one nun made attempts to "test the water" before finally deciding to leave. The decision came only after they were convinced that, in some respects, they were capable of being somebody else, doing something else, or going somewhere else:

> (What influence did such factors—getting a job, dating, making friends—have on your decision to leave?) Until I felt that I could get a job, support myself, pick out clothes, meet new people, I was afraid to leave. I'd be a wierdo, walking

around with a black dress. I wouldn't be a Sister anymore and I'd have to be living off my sixty-year-old mother instead of finding a job. Until I somehow could be convinced that I could do it, I couldn't make the move to decide I could leave. That last year was important to me, then, because I had a job offer, I knew I could go home and live, and I had made new friends; it helped me to think I could do it.

The fact that other nuns had already left also helped to engender confidence in one's ability to do the same. Occasional meetings with former nuns gave respondents some idea of what to expect on the outside and how different former nuns handled a variety of situations. Word would get back indirectly that "so-and-so" was doing fine or was having trouble. In this way, estimates could be made of the degree to which one was prepared to meet the exigencies of leaving:

> (What effect, if any, did other people's leaving have on you?) It encouraged me to leave because you could see that they were making it when they did leave. It encouraged me in the sense that I said, "Well, X left and made it, now Y is happy and made it, and another is doing fine—why can't I make it?" Once you see others making it you compare yourself with them and it encourages you.

In even more subtle ways, cues were exchanged concerning the requisites for leaving:

> Another friend of mine had left and had come back to visit. I had answered the door and she was there and I said to her, "It must have taken a lot of nerve to leave and face the unknown." She said, "Yes, it did take a lot of courage." And she gave me the funniest look—I hadn't said a word to her (about wanting to leave)—and then afterwards I thought, "That's what I need. Just courage—to say this is what I'm doing. That's it!"

Two factors were particularly relevant to the respondent's perceived ability to succeed in the secular society—her age and her motive for leaving. In terms of age, the older respondents were more concerned about giving up the security of the convent for an unknown future. They expressed less confidence in being able to meet eligible men, to get married, and to bear children. They had more doubts about being able to fit into secular peer groups, about the ease with which one can change one's life-style, about receiving family support and assistance, and about starting a new career. As we shall see, these concerns and doubts were not always realistic nor predictive of future events, but insofar as respondents defined their age as a limitation it made the decision to leave a more difficult one than for younger respondents. Two older respondents (35 years and over) comment on the implications of their age:

> (What difference did your age make in coming to the decision to leave?) Well, there are different things. At thirty-nine years of age what's going to happen to you for the rest of your life. "Are you going to find somebody?" "Who's

available at this age?" "Who will your friends be?" These things went through my mind. (When?) As I came closer to knowing that I should leave and had to leave.

* * * * * *

I had been in twenty-five years at that time when I first seriously thought about leaving. (You said it was a very hard decision to make?) It was very hard to make because at my age to say, "How can I go out at the age of forty-three, get a job, change my whole life-style?" "Would I really be able to do it?" Especially at that age! I couldn't rely on my family. Who would my friends be? These things had to be considered.

On the contrary, younger respondents frequently referred to their age as a facilitating factor in making the decision:

I felt that at twenty-six I wouldn't be so different from other girls at my age. I still had time to get married and have children. I could even have a new career if I wanted. This made it easier for me to leave than had I been in longer.

The motives for wanting to leave also colored estimates of one's ability. Those respondents who were being "pulled" by attractive alternatives in the lay world, whose motives were personal, made efforts to embrace new experiences and new relations. They found these rewarding and gained confidence in their ability to meet and master new social situations. The focus of their attention moved toward the future and the secular society that awaited them.

Those whose motive for leaving was ideological, who felt they were being "pushed out" of religious life were less likely to seek and find secular alternatives that they defined as valuable and gratifying. They were still more concerned with the direction religious life was taking than with charting out new pathways for their own passage out of this life. Rather than expressing the often-mentioned pleasures of those who were discovering different parts of themselves and the outside world, they described the bitterness, rage, despair, and frustration that took its toll on them both physically and mentally. One former nun spoke of a nervous breakdown, another of ulcers. Some went for psychological counseling while others lost weight or became ill. Indeed, there is some evidence that these respondents finally decided to leave because they were no longer able, as nuns, to function effectively or feared some type of physical or emotional breakdown:

For myself, I had decided at that point to leave. (What brought you to that decision?) I was really losing my peace of mind. I couldn't sleep, could't eat, was very nervous and upset and I felt it would be better for me, all around, to just get out. There was so much bitterness—so much tension. I was going to a psychologist myself to try to straighten things out and get an objective view of the situation. I began to become neurotic, almost to the point where I was getting a terrible image of myself. I was really disturbed, very upset by the whole situation. That's when I decided to leave. For me, I think it was a push rather than pull. I just had to leave because the situation was so unpleasant for me. Had I my choice, I would have stayed.

Another factor that influenced the perceived ability to leave the religious role had to do with the matter of final vows. For nuns who took final, as opposed to temporary, vows, their ability to perceive themselves as able to leave the religious role depended, to some extent, on their redefinition of the final vows as no longer binding. The taking of final vows, as we mentioned, was a permanent commitment by the nun to religious and community life. It is the last step in the long process of religious socialization and formally symbolizes the community's total and final acceptance of the nun into religious life. Each nun who finally left came to redefine these vows as no longer permanently binding. Rather, it was seen as a commitment that could be appealed and broken with impunity. In this way, she came to feel no moral obligation to remain in religious life, and was safeguarded against feelings of guilt or failure:

> I had to come to terms with the vows, too, and to realize that although when I took them I meant them to be forever, that now they were no longer relevant for me. They were just a formality now. I don't think you could leave unless you really believed that. In fact, I know a few nuns who are still there because they couldn't face breaking the vows.
>
> * * * * * *
>
> The final vows were a big thing for many nuns. It was a major stumbling block that had to be thought through, reexamined. If you really believed the vows were for life, then even if you wanted to leave you couldn't face the decision. I began to rethink the vows as a more temporary commitment that I made earlier in life and could be free from.

So far, we have seen that the decision to voluntarily relinquish a major role is a complex process that involves cognitive and motivational factors as well as estimates of ability. These individual attributes, in turn, are dependent on social factors, both structural and environmental, such as increased access to ways of knowing about alternative roles and life-styles, the opportunity to play these roles and engage in these new modes of living, and getting positive rewards from these experiences. The process of deciding to relinquish a role is thus made up of a sequence of steps in which certain personal and structural factors play off one another at each stage, giving rise to different questions, problems, and solutions. In addition, this sequence is experienced in a dialectical fashion with each step feeding back into the others and shaping them further.

On the basis of our findings at this point we can state some general observations about how social actors arrive at a decision to pass from one to other social locations. The persons making the decision both shape, and in turn are shaped by, the movement through the sequence. Changes in the social system in which their roles are embedded generate a call for assessments of the impact of these changes on the social system itself as well as on the content of the roles available in the system. When certain changes provide opportunities for knowledge about and participation in new activities and in new relationships, people begin to make comparative evaluations between present and possible future modes of living. As they weigh the varying costs and rewards among different alternatives, they seek out more specific and unambiguous cues concerning their ability to leave their present position and move into others. This may involve considerations of the ways in which others respond to the person in such new situations. Receiving rewards for new behavior serves to increase the incentive to make a role change. It also entails what Gouldner (1965) refers to as "anticipatory adaptation" insofar as people become aware of the requisites for leave-taking by interacting with those who have already done so. In addition, we note that people redefine the meanings of certain events (in this study, for example, taking final vows) to reduce feelings of guilt or failure. As Bredemeier and Stephenson note (1962, p.101), a role passage may be facilitated by reducing the feelings of guilt that a person may experience as a cost of changing roles.

We can now proceed to integrate additional dimensions of the process of relinquishment with what we have already uncovered. Specifically, leaving a major role also involves "rehearsals" for leaving, strategies for setting the time and manner of disengagement from the role, and the development of acceptable explanations for relinquishment. In the next two chapters we will examine the ways in which these additional themes are played out and assess their consequences for this and the subsequent phases of the overall passage.

4

Rehearsals

Sociologists use the term "anticipatory socialization" to refer to the process of learning about the values, norms, and orientations of social roles before one actually assumes them. This process of anticipatory learning and acquisition consists of "rehearsals" that help prepare the social actor for playing a new role in life. In the drama that is everyday life, these rehearsals are quite familiar to us. Children play house, medical students "go on rounds," there is an engagement period prior to marriage, we attend wakes and funerals. All serve, either intentionally or not, to help us prepare for the future roles we will or must play.

The same is true for those nuns who were thinking of leaving religious life while still in the convent. They, too, began to rehearse some of the roles that they would be expected to play in the lay world. Certain of these preparations were *intentional* on their part and reflect the *deliberate* attempt by persons to consciously shape their ability to move into new roles. Other opportunities for rehearsal, however, were the *unintended* and *unanticipated* consequence of ongoing changes occurring in religious life. Once again, the long-standing sociological tradition of looking beyond the apparent and intended results of human action yields significant insights into the complexity of social behavior. What were some of these unintended opportunities for rehearsing future roles?

One of them centered around modifications of the religious dress or habit worn by nuns. As we mentioned, debate among nuns over what form the habit should take was very intense. Eventually this order gave permission for nuns to experiment with different dress variations. Whether nuns chose a skirt and blouse or dress, the change from the traditional black habit resulted in making more of the woman visible—her hair, her physique, her legs, and arms. To assess the implication of this change in habit we must understand some of the consequences of uniforms. In a significant article, Joseph and Alex (1972, pp.719–730) discuss the uniform as a device for identifying group members and ordering the priorities of role obligations for the individual. The traditional habit was a symbol, for the nun and for outsiders, of membership in a particular group. Her reception of the habit after the novitiate year was symbolic of her admission to the religious order as well as a basis for changing her self-conception from lay person to "Sister." The habit, which was worn at virtually all times both in the convent and outside, was a constant reminder of one's religious role and served to channel other people's responses to her. As Joseph and Alex note (1972):

> The uniform influences the wearer himself, for everyone is an other who proffers the same mirror. Since no other statuses, or any touch of individuality, are recognized in the uniformed individual by others, he is encouraged to act primarily as an occupant of his uniformed status.   (p.726)

The respondent was, then, at all times and for all others—herself included—primarily a nun. This was her "master status" symbolically confirmed by the habit. Just as changes in other areas of religious life were intended to renew and increase the viability of religious life, so too were changes in the habit intended to encourage more "open" access and "genuine" response between nuns and others. This indeed happened, but not always with the intended results.

The modified habit demanded that nuns pay more attention to matters of appearance, clothing styles, personal habits, and skills:

> Because you were in the modified habit you learned some of the ways to dress and what new things were coming out. I even had to shave my legs and set my hair. I tried to lose some weight too. You don't realize how flabby you got until you got out of those twenty pounds of clothes.
> * * * * * *
> I was teaching girls at the time and they were very conscious of what we were wearing. I remember one day going in and I had gotten new shoes and had shortened my habit and one of the kids said to me, "You're getting there." So, you knew kids were looking at every change. The mothers, too, told me the new habit had nice lines and made me look thin. I began to have a much better self-image than before.

Every respondent indicated that the new habit had an impact on the salience of her sex-role identification. In some cases it helped to sustain and revive her awareness of herself as a woman. In other instances it actually generated this awareness.

> We were allowed to wear colored blouses and dresses after a while and then when we took off the veil too it was the kind of thing where I said, "My gosh! I know I'm a woman!" It was, "Wow!" For me, being a woman was now more evident—pronounced.
> * * * * * *

(You said the change in habit helped you to be more aware of yourself as a woman—could you explain that?) I guess I had reached the point where I didn't subconsciously want to be an "it" anymore. I had been an "it"—a neuter being and shedding the habit, the outward manifestations of "it," helped me to see myself as a woman.

Other people also began to change their responses to the nun in the modified habit. This in turn reinforced her image of herself as a woman:

Getting out of that habit really did start things off. On a teasing basis, men would begin to respond to you as a woman. That sort of reaffirmed you as a woman. Most people responded to you as a neuter gender and now here were men who were overlooking the fact that you were a nun and responded to you as a woman.

Changes in the habit, then, began to alter the nun's image of herself as a woman and her way of relating to other people. It changed the manner in which she presented herself to others and the kinds of reactions others had toward her. Also, by appearing in clothes that more closely approximated secular dress, the nun was able to ease herself into public roles and acquire some familiarity with secular routines:

With the traditional habit you were always conspicuous when you were out. People could identify you. With the modified habit you could slip into the outside world as a regular person and it helped you to become more comfortable as a normal, regular person. You didn't stick out anymore.

The respondents mentioned the pleasure of being able to move unnoticed in everyday circles—shopping, browsing, attending meetings, going to classes— and being treated "like everyone else." In this way, nuns had greater opportunity to pick up the small routines and skills of secular living and to practice and refine them in unobtrusive ways.

These ramifications of changes in the habit also had an impact on the imagery with which respondents identified themselves. New "selves" were opening up. Being a nun became just one of a number of existential possibilities. As these nuns became more aware of what else they could be, what selves were latently subsumed under their role as nuns, their close identification with the religious role diminished. As one perceptive respondent recalls:

I thought we would lose our identity (with a change in the habit). I realized afterwards the psychological change it had for me in terms of identity. It had a terrific change. Men would comment on our appearance. People began to become more open with us.

Respondents made frequent references to the effect of the change in habit in facilitating their development as "persons." They believed that they were responded to as "individuals" in their own right, rather than merely role players. They felt that their new relations to others were more "genuine," "open," "free." This reaction is not surprising, because uniforms do function to suppress "individual idiosyncracies in behavior and appearance" (Joseph & Alex, 1972, p.723) as well as in self-image. Indeed, one respondent recalled that many nuns strove to assert their individuality by manipulating their appearance in the choice of color, cut, style, and texture of their clothing. Changes in habit, then, gave respondents the chance to try on new "selves," to activate latent roles, and to rehearse behaviors and attitudes that would be called for when they left. In effect, these changes served as opportunities for respondents to perceive themselves as something other than religious women. At the same time it provided an occasion for the rehearsal of future statuses and roles.

Other opportunities for rehearsal came by way of the nun's greater access to the secular world. Although the purpose of allowing nuns such freedom was to enhance their ability to serve others as a witness to Christ in the world, a consequence of increased exposure to lay life was the chance to learn about and practice different roles. Four respondents reflect on their experiences at rehearsals:

> The last year I was in (religious life) we went to so many parties and although it's not like going while you're out, we related to people on a social level. I had a chance to learn how to carry myself.
>
> * * * * * *
>
> When I was in that convent, things began to really get loose and we had a lot of freedom. I began to read, watch TV, go to movies, and just get back into the swing of things. By the time I left I was pretty well tuned into what was happening outside.
>
> * * * * * *
>
> I was living on campus during the summer and it was hard, at first, accepting the freedom, but I came to be friendly with three girls in the dormitory and went to meals with them and we started doing things together. They had a car and we'd go out and sometimes I forgot I was a nun.
>
> * * * * * *
>
> We would go into New York on our own and I was involved with parish groups and the kids and I think that was some kind of preparation because it wasn't like a woman coming out of a cloister and all of a sudden there's the world.

As these comments suggest, the increased exposure to the outside world—through the media, graduate school, participation in groups and organizations—provided a chance for nuns to learn about social changes occurring in the secular society. It also allowed them to anticipate the expectations of the new roles that they would play.

Another source of anticipatory preparation was the romantic and sexual involvement of some nuns while they were still in the convent. Thirteen of the respondents indicated they were romantically involved with men, and seven of those had some sexual encounters as well. No clear differences emerge between respondents who did and did not become involved in some manner with men. I had expected that involvements might be related at least to the nun's age or the type of vow taken but this did not hold true. The only clear pattern that appeared is that, with one exception, the men with whom the respondents became involved were priests. It is important to note that during this time of renewal in religious orders friendships with priests were strongly encouraged in many circles as part of the attempt to help religious men and women deal with their own personhood and sex status.[1] Relations between priests and nuns that ranged from platonic friendship to romantic love were frequent. They were well known at least in religious circles, and suspected among the public at large.[2]

While nuns were always in minimal association with lay males and, to a greater extent with priests, their interactions prior to the sixties were strictly regulated and monitored. However, in the spirit of openness that shaped the changes in religious life the frequency and the quality of contact permitted between nuns and priests in particular began to change. The opportunities for nuns to meet and work with priests increased. They would be found together at parish meetings, on college campuses, at summer institutes, and inner-city programs. Unlike the highly restricted, formalized encounters between priests and nuns in earlier times, the wave of liberalizing change provided an atmosphere in which certain priests and nuns could come together in more spontaneous, informal, and personal ways. For some respondents, relations with priests were limited to friendship. For them it was the first time since entering religious life that they had the chance to have male friends:

> He and I were just friends and it was so good to be able to have a man friend— just to be comfortable with a man as a man. It was something I hadn't done since high school and at first it was hard, but I got used to it very quickly.

For other nuns, friendship turned to romantic love and, in some cases, physical involvement. Most respondents greeted this turn of events with ambivalence. There was both the exhilarating pleasure of deep emotional encounter and the guilt and anxiety over a forbidden relationship.

> (Before the Cursillo I had always had a priest–nun relationship.) It was always sort of proper. Well, you know how nuns used to act toward priests. They were God Almighty and you would turn the house upside down when they came for breakfast. It was after the Cursillo that I became involved with the priest. I went to confession and told the priest that after I went to the Cursillo I really felt like a woman. It was the whole experience—and when you've finished making it everybody comes out and embraces you. Ahh! That was fun! All of a sudden you realized that it felt nice to have a man's arms around you besides your father's. It really felt good. I went to confession and said to Father that I didn't know just what to tell him, but I just felt much more open—he knew I had made

---

[1] See, for example, Suenens (1962) and Muckenhirn (1967).

[2] For an account of how a romantic involvement between a priest and nun may lead to their role relinquishment see Jehenson (1969).

the Cursillo—and I feel much more like a woman. It had stirred something in me. (What was his reaction?) He thought it was great. He had made a Cursillo and I'm sure it affected him the same way. Then I went to see him a couple of times after that and it got sort of involved. I'm sure it was like a kid who has fallen in love. (Did you think you were in love with him?) Oh Yes! (Did it become a sexual relationship?) To a certain extent yes. (To what extent?) You know, there was some physical contact. (How did you feel about this new type of relationship?) Well, when we began to play games a little bit that did bother me. I said, "My God!" and then I was running around looking for others, saying "What priest could I go to?" (To go to?) To tell this to. (Why did it bother you?) I'm sure I had been hung-up on sex for a long time. I had been taught that impure thoughts were mortal sins and that I had begun to change some of my thoughts on all this, but I thought that *these* were bad sins—especially with a priest—so I was really bothered about it.

It should be emphasized that these romantic involvements with men came *after* respondents had already begun to evaluate their role in religious life and to contemplate leaving. These involvements, then, were not "the cause" of their leaving. Rather, they can be viewed as a measure of the extent to which strong religious proscriptions had already lessened their impact on these nuns. Respondents who were both emotionally and physically involved with someone indicated that these relationships had an impact on their desire to leave. However, the impact was indirect; that is, they came to experience and enjoy a type of relationship which would be denied them as long as they remained nuns. Not one of the twenty respondents indicated that she left because she was in love with a particular man, or that this particular involvement was "the" overriding reason for leaving; rather, it became one of a number of motives for leaving. It was an opportunity to be involved with others in ways that came to be valued—as lovers, spouses, and parents. It is commonly believed in some circles that nuns left religious life primarily for romantic and sexual reasons. Specifically this explanation suggests that the desire to marry, generated by the romantic involvement of nuns with priests and secular males, led to their decision to leave religious life. Neither my data nor that of others (Ebaugh, 1977, p. 111) lend support to this belief. Obviously, for specific nuns this was the major reason for leaving, but for the majority it was but one of a number of causal factors in their decision to leave. My own impression is that this "explanation" for why nuns left is centered on a sexist vision of women as essentially fulfilled only when they have romantic, sexual, and marital ties to men.

The consequences of such involvements were multiple. First, they emphasized more strongly the fact that the respondents were women and encouraged them to think of themselves and respond to others as women. As one respondent observes, "the relation with the priest helped me a great deal in realizing that I was a woman and was attractive as such to men." The involvements also brought into sharp focus the romantic and sexual dimensions of the persons that were suppressed and denied in religious roles

(Jehenson, 1969, p. 296). Respondents now had opportunities to relate to men as *women,* to learn or brush up on emotional and sexual responses, to see themselves as sexual beings:

> Having this relationship with that priest before I left helped me become used to men romantically. It gave me more confidence to be with men and I really enjoy men now.
>
> * * * * * *
>
> I learned lots of things—things I never knew before. (What sort of things?) Sexual and romantic aspects of relationships. (Was this your first romantic and sexual experience?) Yes, it was very new to me. There were things I had to learn. You don't know if you're doing the right thing, not morally, but insofar as pleasing the other person sexually.

These opportunities for sex-role rehearsal and experimentation cushioned the adjustments that were to be made upon leaving the convent. Here were chances to learn, practice, and anticipate the expectations of sex roles and romantic encounters. Although, as we will show, a number of factors are related to postconvent dating and marriage patterns (for example, length of time out, types of friends), the respondents who were married or frequently dating all had some emotional or physical involvement while in the convent. This pattern strongly suggests that these encounters did facilitate the movement to sex roles and romantic relationships.

Two other unintended sources of preparation for postconvent experiences can also be briefly explored. Both of them, again, were consequences of the changes being made in religious communities. Prior to Vatican Council II it was not unusual for nuns to be teaching without having a college degree, and very few nuns had postgraduate training. Part of the renewal effort was a call for improved educational opportunities for nuns along with encouragement to assume jobs in the secular marketplace. These changes meant that nuns became better educated more quickly than before. They were exposed to new perspectives, role models, and reference groups. Some accumulated experience in secular jobs and became colleagues of lay persons. These changes meant that, especially for the younger nuns, their chances of having finished college before leaving the convent were greatly increased. In addition, their years of teaching and experience in other occupational positions would be counted by secular employers in assessing their suitability for jobs and salary levels once they left religious life. Indeed, all twenty respondents left having already received their college degree and had a number of years of teaching experience behind them. Some had finished a graduate degree and had experience in inner-city employment. These factors obviously made it much easier to obtain a job and command a reasonable salary. Indeed, all but three respondents had secured a job within weeks after leaving religious life. Unwittingly, then, these improved educational and occupational opportunities served, for some nuns, to better prepare them for taking their position in the secular labor market.

In addition to these changes, nuns were also encouraged to take on more responsibility in carrying out the variety of tasks required to manage a convent house. In earlier times these tasks were given to the local superior who then allocated specific functions to each member of the house. As communities began to delegate such responsibilities and as new convents were opened these opportunities were available not only to the older nuns with more seniority but to some younger ones as well. A younger respondent recalls:

> We were very free and had nobody to account to. We had a car. I had complete control over all the finances. We were buying things and learning how to handle money and that was a very good learning experience for us, so that wasn't a really big concern when I left.

Many respondents recalled the various opportunities to do shopping for the convent house, make purchases, deal with service people, handle money, balance budgets, and a whole range of household activities. They were beginning to acquire the more mundane skills of the secular world that would turn out to be profitable once they left the convent. For the other respondents without these experiences their accommodations to shopping, banking, budgeting, and dealing with service people took longer and required more effort once they assumed secular roles. One respondent noted during the interview that she had never had a checking account and found it embarrassing to appear so naïve at the bank. Another remarked on how long it took her to learn to handle budgeting and shopping. Thus, for a young woman who had entered religious life immediately after high school, and spent five or more years in a role that limited her familiarity with routine consumer skills and roles, unless she had access to these activities while in the convent her subsequent adjustment upon leaving would be more difficult for her.

Up to this point we have concentrated on the unanticipated consequences of changes occurring in religious life during the late sixties. We have observed the irony of how, for some nuns, these changes resulted not in a renewed commitment to the religious role but rather in an increased desire to abandon it. Their exposure to alternative life-styles inadvertently served to enhance their desire to leave and subtly prepared them for making their exit.

Once the respondents had made the decision to leave, they began to make more *intentional* preparations for moving into the secular world. These deliberate efforts to prepare for future role demands highlights the active person-in-transit who is aware and can take control of some of the exigencies of role passage. What kinds of preparations did these former nuns make? How did they influence the decision to leave? Why were some viewed as more important than others? We turn now to these questions and begin by examining the nun's relation to her parents and family.

Of all the ways in which these women tried to ease their exit from religious life one loomed large in importance and priority—preparing their parents for their decision to leave. Every one of the twenty women participated in this mode of preparation. In a few cases it was only a matter of weeks before, but more usually it was many months prior to leaving that the respondent informed her family of her decision. This was a crucial step in the relinquishment process, in part because the anticipated responses from their families colored their own feelings about leaving and their expectations about what would confront them after they left. Every woman indicated that her parents' reactions to her decision was of special significance. All respondents hoped their parents would understand the decision and be able to accept it. They wanted to "cushion the shock" of their leaving by preparing them in advance. They wanted their parents' trust, if not approval, that this was a mature and responsible choice; they hoped that their families would support them emotionally and, as one said "Even if I didn't want to go live with them, it was a comforting thought that they would want you back, that you had someplace to go, that somebody cared."

With one exception, all respondents reported that their parents were generally positive, sympathetic, and supportive of their decision. A typical encounter is described by one respondent:

> My parents knew that something was wrong because I was complaining about things more frequently. Once when I went home my mother said, "If I were you, I'd quit that whole thing. They're working you too hard." I felt like saying, "This is what I've come to tell you." I was so nervous about telling them, so I waited almost the whole weekend and couldn't tell them. The last day we were having supper and I thought, "I have to say something." So I said, "Would the two of you be very upset if I took a year's leave of absence?" My father said, "Hell no!" and my mother said, "I think it'd be great!" And boy! Did I ever feel relieved.

Other parents had mixed reactions. A point not often emphasized in discussions of role passage is the fact then when a person relinquishes a role it has consequences for the roles that others play and their relationship to the person who is leaving a role. The parents of nuns are a case in point. Some respondents reported receiving a certain amount of negative reaction to their decision. One set of parents, for example, expressed a loss of reflected prestige that they enjoyed while their daughter was a nun:

> Initially it upset them a little to think I was leaving. You know, it was a status symbol too in a way. "My daughter the nun" sort of thing. Although they never wanted me to enter, once they adjusted to it my father would light up with pride when talking about his daughter the nun.

Other parents expressed concern over being responsible again, as parents, for their daughter and the adjustments that they might have to make in their life style when she left:

> (Did your parents have any other reaction to telling them you were leaving?) My mother was concerned because all of a sudden they had to worry about me again. It was their idea. I had been taken care of all these years and now they had to worry again because I wasn't being taken care of.
> * * * * * *
> My parents had learned to live without me; they had their own life, and I could sense some concern over readjusting to my leaving and come home. (In what way?) Well, even such small things as putting my room back together again, finding a place for my junk, things like that.

Of all the leave-taking preparations, informing one's parents was the most emotionally laden and the most important personally. Every respondent was faced with this issue. Although only one respondent encountered strong parental resistance (she stayed in another year before being able to face them with a determined, positive decision) the interviews clearly suggest that parental reaction was a significant factor in actually leaving. None of the respondents said that they would have changed their minds had their parents disapproved of the decision; however, it was an important factor in the ease with which the decision was made.[3] A former nun comments:

> I think that the greatest factor in making my decision was that I didn't have any fears telling my family. They always took the position that whatever decision we made they would stand by it, so I didn't have to worry about telling my family and what they would think. That may seem crazy to you, but other people are still in because they couldn't face their family—and it's still going on.

In understanding the influence of parental reaction on the decision to leave three distinct dimensions must be considered. One is the *anticipated* response made by parents to the decision to leave religious life; the second is the *actual* reaction by parents to the decision; and third, the *importance* placed on parental approval. If persons have strong needs for parental approval, then anticipated or actual responses of a disapproving nature may change the decision, or at least postpone it. More generally, relinquishing roles is more likely to occur when significant others, as reference groups, provide approval or support for relinquishment. In the case of our nuns, parents remained a most significant reference group although other sources of approval were provided by respondents' close friends, nuns who had left, and ideological groups. The great importance placed on parental approval suggests that

---

[3]In studying priests who leave the priesthood, Jehenson (1969) also notes the impact of family response: "A priest's father and mother are frequently responsible for his decision not to leave the religious system because he fears breaking emotional ties with them or causing them grief" (p. 299).

religious life retards the development of independence from family and forestalls the emergence of mature, autonomous persons. As Hyman (1959, pp. 98–109) noted, deferring to parental authority, the need for parental approval, and the significance of parental attitudes and values declines with age. In the normal course of personal development parents are usually replaced by other groups as sources of approval, support, and respect. Yet these respondents, all of them *chronologically* in adult age roles, express concern for parental approval more appropriate for persons at much younger ages and stages of maturation. The traditional structure of religious life, its stress on collectivity, hierarchy, obedience, and ideological and behavioral conformity had produced women who were emotionally and socially much younger than their actual age would suggest.[4] That the respondents themselves were increasingly aware of this will be discussed at length in a later chapter.

Another frequent intentional preparation for postconvent life was oriented toward employment and financial stability. Many respondents made efforts to acquaint themselves with the job market, to establish contacts with outsiders concerning possible employment, or actually to go on job interviews while still in religious life. A few respondents even had jobs waiting for them by the time they left. For most respondents this would be their first foray into the labor market and some utilized various resources to try to smooth the transition into occupational roles. They searched the "want" ads for possible jobs; others helped them to write up resumes; former nuns advised on openings at their place of employment, or suggested appropriate salary levels; they evaluated possible "interview" behavior—what to say about one's religious affiliation, how to field employers' questions, and what to wear. On the whole, these efforts were sporadic and unsystematic and many respondents left the convent with a rather incomplete set of expectations, skills, and information for moving into the job market. Nonetheless, for those who did anticipate in some way the demands of employment their adjustment to new work roles was that much easier once they left. They took less time to find a job, felt more comfortable on job interviews, negotiated more favorable salaries and benefits, and were less likely to mention job adjustment as the most difficult part of the overall transition.

The area of preparation over which respondents had most control was their own physical appearance. We have already mentioned the effects of the change in religious habit on the respondents' general appearance, personal skills, and the like. What the modified habit did in one respect was make the woman somewhat less easily identifiable as a nun. However, there were still

---

[4]It could be argued that self-selection of certain types of young women to religious life accounts for their socioemotional immaturity. Even if this is so, the very structure of religious community inhibited rather than facilitated maturation.

very visible physical clues that signaled her religious role to others. In commenting on this cluster of signals, one respondent observes that even when nuns went into more secular clothing styles "the clothes were very dowdy, conservative, and too large for them. Their hairstyles were not in fashion and now you could see how out-of-shape many of them had become—they were fat or flabby." However, some respondents had retained their interest in fashion styles and trends while in the convent and had not significantly changed in physical appearance since entering religious life. Their efforts at preparation consisted mainly of buying some clothing, shoes, and accessories currently in fashion by reading magazines, observing their students' attire, and sewing clothes for themselves. For others the physical task was greater. They let their hair grow or styled it differently, went on diets, exercised, and attempted to get into the swing of clothes shopping and other personal purchases. Four women describe these efforts:

> I remember that the first thing I bought was what I call my "go to an interview dress." When I think back on it now, I laugh. (Why is that?) It was one of those knit type of suits like little old women wear. I don't think I would wear it now, but at that time I didn't know better. And then I wore gloves, which weren't even in style then—but how did I know? (How did you know what was in style?) I began to look in the papers, look at the ads, which before I had no reason to do.
> * * * * * *
> Before I decided to leave I kept my hair short—very short—and I didn't want to go out looking weird so I started to let it grow and by the time I left it was a reasonable length.
> * * * * * *
> I knew I was going to leave and I couldn't weigh one hundred and seventy-five pounds when I left. I went on a diet and lost sixty pounds by the time I had left. Also, I began to be consciously interested in what I would look like in the middle of that last year. I watched what other people had on, how they put their clothes together.
> * * * * * *
> I communicated to my friends that I needed time to just get used to walking in a store, and funny things like that. I needed time to get used to going into a bargain basement and dressing in a public dressing room.

A few respondents made no effort to alter their physical appearance. The reasons they gave included their preoccupation with other issues or areas of relinquishment, the short length of time between their decision to leave and actually leave-taking and their desire to wait until coming out before making any further changes. For most respondents, interest in physical appearance was less important before, than after, they left. With other issues such as job, residence, and family taking up more of their concern, time, and energies, they were satisfied with moderate alterations in appearance. It was only after they were out that what they looked like came to be of more significance. This became important as a means of controlling biographical information, as a way of blending into the social landscape, and as a personal index of successful management of the passage.

The most immediate practical concern upon leaving was where to reside. Many options were not actually feasible because of the lack of money for rent, furniture, or a car and the absence of a job. The initial options basically were going back home to live with one's family or to room with one or more former nuns who had already left or were leaving at about the same time. Virtually no one could afford to live alone or had maintained friendships with outsiders with whom they could live.

The majority of respondents decided to go back to their family's residence. Their reasons varied. For a few, going home was viewed as a temporary or necessary stopping off point. These women were going to get married, going away to graduate school, planning to move out of the area for job reasons, or wanted to accumulate enough money to eventually be able to move out. They did not intend to remain at home and this expectation mader it easier to deal with some of the difficulties that arose later on between respondent and kin. Other respondents reported that they went home because this seemed to be the best all around choice. They got along with their parents; they felt they could have as much freedom as they wanted; this was financially the best arrrangement; or, there was no one else they wanted to live with at the time. Adjustments to family relations, as we will discuss later, were more difficult for them in part because the tolerance that comes from knowing a situation is temporary was less available to them. A smaller number of respondents did not decide to go home. Instead they chose to room with another former nun, or joined a larger group of women who had left the convent. No respondent initially chose to live alone.

Choice of residence was an important one with implications for different phases of the overall passage. On the other hand, moving home was the closest approximation to the familial environment of the convent. It was also the place where one could receive emotional support from those who knew you best and with whom you felt most at ease. At home one could recoup, be in a familiar network of relations, routine, and place; the family would provide service, assistance, information, and financial support. In this sense choice of family residence could be a cushion to absorb the more emotionally charged aspects of leaving and initial accommodations. Of equal importance, going home could decrease the interaction one had with other former nuns and force the respondent to come to terms with people, routines, expectations, and roles that were not part of her religious life. Family residence can be seen, then, as serving "degrouping" functions (Merton, 1968, p. 328) similar to other organizations (halfway houses, dormitories, outpatient clinics, replacement depots) that facilitate passages by de-emphasizing old ties and building up new ones. One respondent, who declined an offer to join a group of former nuns and instead decided to go home, comments:

(Why did you decide not to live with them?) It just seemed to me that I would be leaving one thing I really didn't want anymore and going into this other little group where we would all be together again. It just seemed like you would never get away from all that—the convent stuff—unless you really got out of it.

A final mode of intended preparation centered on one's age peers in the outside world. This type of preparation was more available to the younger respondents because they were more likely than older respondents to have a peer group whose roles and range of experience was more accessible to them. For example, younger respondents had friends who were still single, had completed college, and were not yet firmly established in a certain life-style. Older respondents, first of all, were less likely to have retained contact with their former friends. Also, their age peers were likely to be married, raising children, and embedded in a social network of work and friendships. The younger respondents contacted friends they had known before entering, or had developed while in religious life, told them of their decision to leave and made plans to "get together" or "do things" after they had left. They were aware of the ways in which these friends could pave the way for them in such areas of social life, friendship, practical suggestions, and the like. One respondent began going home on weekends to spend time with lay friends "knowing that this would be a good thing for me to do so I would have something to go to when I actually left." In another instance, a respondent went shopping, to the movies, and sporting events with two of her lay friends "to begin to make links to the real world with regular people, not nuns or priests or anybody connected with the Church." At least for younger women, then, reestablishing social ties with secular friends helped to ease their passage out of religious life by orienting themselves to the future and to different reference groups. This discussion of anticipatory socialization, both unintended and deliberate, suggests it is difficult to delineate with much precision when relinquishment actually takes place. For some time before the last day they were officially members of the religious order, these women were in varying degrees already withdrawing from the religious role. Different identities and roles were being activated; new skills and knowledge were acquired; alternate bases of interaction were tested; appearance was modified; and new selves were presented. As one respondent astutely observes, "I think I was out (of religious life) before I actually left." This, of course, is not dissimilar to the marriage that dies sometime before the divorce or the student who drops out before actually leaving school. The point being underscored here is that relinquishment involves not only learning and adopting new behaviors and attitudes but also learning to relinquish prior ones (Riley et al., 1972, p. 537). Past behaviors, definitions, relations, and expectations come to be viewed as less rewarding and valuable, thus providing additional incentives to relinquish the role.

Respondents, as they moved closer and closer to the decision to leave, increasingly withdrew from prescribed religious activities, norms, beliefs, and values. What was once rewarding came to be perceived in more negative terms. Their extent of deviation from religious expectations and roles was rather broad. They stopped going to Mass and common prayer on a regular basis, they wore secular clothes while at home, they went out without permission, smoked cigarettes, had romantic involvements, and failed to attend community meetings among others.

In addition to these *behavioral* violations of rules and expectations, respondents also began to hold beliefs and meanings at odds with official ones. These ranged from the extremes of doubting the existence of God, the validitiy of the sacraments, and the efficacy of prayer, to rejecting the authority of the heads of religious orders and the belief in the necessity of "community life," positing the existence of a "temporary" vocation and a denial of the binding nature and meaning of final vows. Situations, events, rules, and expectations that once were valued came to be defined as arbitrary, "silly," meaningless, and harmful. These women had abandoned their commitment to aspects of official religious ideology and the structures that sustain them.

These violations of norms and shifts in belief were aided and encouraged by changes in respondents' role models and reference groups:

> I used to look up to the older Sisters as my model—they were what I thought I should be in the sense of being holy, obedient, not critical, pure. You know, the good nun. But I came to see that they were not necessarily doing these things for the right reason. They were conditioned to be this way without examining the value of it. A group of us would talk a lot about this and now I reject that way of living, of being. You have to decide for yourself what is right for you, for those you come in contact with, for the community. The so-called radicals were trying to make this point earlier, but I didn't see it then—now I understand what they were trying to do.

Through discussions with others, comparisons between groups, and evaluations of alternatives their allegiances began to shift, new role models emerged, and different reference groups provided standards for appropriate beliefs, attitudes, and activity. Thus, respondents were not only beginning to orient themselves to postconvent life; they were also disengaging themselves from the religious role, finding it less and less rewarding over time.

Violations of role expectations may also serve as a clue to possible role relinquishment, both for oneself and others. These signals or clues can range from those that are subtle and less visible to more overt and obvious ones:

> (Can you tell that someone is thinking of leaving?) Certainly, if you knew them well. You can see them changing their pattern of acting—the way they talk and feel about things. There's a certain anxiety that comes through.
>
> * * * * * *
>
> (Were you able to tell that some people were thinking about leaving?) Yes. They began to cut themselves off from an active involvement in the community. You could almost see themselves physically throw up their hands and say they had it! (Was there anything else?) Some of them became sick. Others became so

involved with people on the outside that you could see that they were making some kind of pre-inroads and paving their way for when they would leave.

Respondents also interpreted these signs not only as indicators that others may be contemplating leaving, but also that they themselves were moving toward relinquishment:

> I stopped going to community meetings. That was a really big thing—once you stopped going to meetings that was it! You knew you were on the way out and so did everybody else.

* * * * * *

> When I started to lose a lot of weight and couldn't sleep and was very irritable, I knew that things were really getting bad. You could see it happening to others and now it was happening to me. I began to wonder just how long I would be able to go like this without actually leaving.

As the above quotes indicate, "insiders" were highly sensitive to specific cues which they recognize as signals of possible relinquishment. Their intimate knowledge of religious life enabled them to pick up hints and clues that outsiders were not aware of. Outsiders, nevertheless, were also able to detect changes in the nuns that suggested they might be considering leaving the convent. As I mentioned earlier, many parents were not that surprised upon hearing of their daughter's decision to leave. Such signals as the increasing frequency of home visits and critical comments about convent life, among other changes in behavior, were interpreted by them that not all was well. Three women reflect on this phenomenon:

> (Are there signs that people are leaving or thinking about it?) Yes, I think so. I think that that's how my mother could see it. I would start going home in lay clothes, which she was very surprised at. "Oh! can you wear that?" "No, but so what?" Well, I was never like this and she knew that, but she never said a word; she wasn't surprised.

* * * * * *

> My mother knew that something was bothering me because I used to come home and talk about what was going on in the community in more negative ways, something I never would have done before.

* * * * * *

> One of my closest friends began to get suspicious about my plans to leave when she would see how indifferent I was becoming to being home at a certain hour, or doing things without getting permission.

In this way, of course, others were being prepared for possible relinquishment and given time to contemplate the difference it would make for them. Unwittingly, respondents themselves were acting as anticipatory socialization agents, providing the opportunity for others to begin making accommodations to different types of relationships.[5]

---

[5]For another example of how persons involved in role transitions unintentionally provide opportunities for role rehearsal, see Deutscher's (1962) discussion of the emergent postparental transition.

Some summary comments on rehearsals are in order at this point. As we shall see in later chapters, those nuns who engaged in more rehearsals while still in the convent were more likely to report less difficulty in making the passage to secular life and to have acquired a greater array of roles in the outside world. Our findings reveal that rehearsals, practical preparations, and anticipatory learning facilitate the passage to new roles and life-styles.[6]

In this chapter we have also seen how persons who are negotiating an emergent passage are forced to rely on their own resources to anticipate and prepare for future roles. In well-established passages relinquishment is guided by customs, rituals, and rules that help ease the person out of her or his role with minimal strain and confusion. Emergent passages lack, by their very nature, these institutionalized rehearsals and conventional modes of anticipatory socialization. This fact makes greater demands on the individual to become an active agent in preparing for relinquishment and the acquisition of future roles. The way in which these preparations are made, their efficacy and consequences for subsequent phases of the passage offer a rich set of theoretical problems that should encourage further sociological inquiry.

---

[6]Our hypothesis that role rehearsal facilitates role passage supports similar findings in other research. For example, Deutscher's (1962) work on adjustment to altered family roles and Ellis and Lane's (1967) study of accommodations to college life specifically focus on anticipatory socialization as a major factor in transitional adjustments.

5

Strategies for Leaving

As we have seen, relinquishing a social role is a fluid, complex process involving, in part, motives, meanings, relationships, and rehearsals. There are two additional dimensions of disengaging from a role that demand our attention. The first has to do with choosing among alternative paths away from a role. Virtually all exits from a role may be accomplished in more than one way and each option carries with it different meanings and consequences for the person leaving a role. For example, the potential exits from a marriage include emotional withdrawal, separation, divorce, and desertion. Reflecting on the alternative ways to leave marriage, employment, psychotherapy, and schooling illustrates the wide range of choices and constraints, sentiments and consequences that surround different modes of role exit.

Nuns who had taken perpetual or final vows could choose among three official pathways out of religious life. A dispensation from vows could be granted to a nun by the Sacred Congregation for Religious in Rome; receiving a dispensation thus terminated all legal and religious ties between the nun and her order and resulted in a permanent withdrawal from religious life. The other two pathways—a leave of absence and an exclaustration—were temporary withdrawals from the order in which a specified amount of time was granted to a nun during which she could evaluate her vocation and motivation to be a nun. These temporary withdrawals required the nun to remain faithful to her vows. However, a leave of absence was a less severe withdrawal because, unlike exclaustration, a nun on leave could wear the religious habit, hold office, and vote in the order. In either case, the nun was released from a variety of convent rules and was free to live with lay people in secular society for a specified time period. Nuns who had taken temporary, as opposed to final, vows could be permanently released from religious life by the order itself without being granted formal dispensation from Rome. Of course, any nun who wanted to leave without receiving official permission from any source could do so. However, this was a rarely chosen form of exit for reasons ranging from its social impropriety to the fact that failure to receive dispensation from final vows may pose religious limitations on certain options, such as the right to get married in the church.

Parenthetically, it should be noted that the order itself had the authority to either grant a leave of absence to the nun or demand that she apply to the Sacred Congregation for an exclaustration. The order, in addition, reserved the right to ask that a nun request a leave before seeking final dispensation or to refuse to grant a leave and demand application for dispensation. This authority points up the fact that even in self-initiated role relinquishment official agents may be able to exert some control over both the type of exit from a role and its timing.

What was the pattern of role exit for our sample of former nuns? Of the twenty, all but three initially requested a temporary leave of absence; two respondents asked for a permanent dispensation and the other woman was denied request for a leave and "was forced to get a dispensation because I was a radical troublemaker." In the earlier stages of the research I had expected that the choice of exit would be associated with other variables such as the type of vow taken, the number of years spent in religious life, the type of motivation for leaving, the certainty of the motive, and the amount of anticipatory rehearsal for leaving. Specifically, I anticipated that requests for dispensations—a permanent and complete severance of bonds with the order—would come from nuns with temporary vows; who had spent fewer years in religious life; whose motive for leaving was personal, not ideological; who was more certain of her desire to leave; and who had taken more opportunities for rehearsing secular roles. Why, then, did these expected relationships fail to materialize?[1]

In analyzing the data I began to search for other explanations for the consistent pattern of request for leaves of absence. Of special interest to me were the nine cases where the respondents requested a leave even though they were very certain of their desire to permanently abandon religious life and expressed no intention of being bound to the community by their vows during their leave. Why would these women, sure of their wish to relinquish religious life and already expressing minimal intention to strictly obey their vows and other obligations while on leave, not simply request a dispensation? This was the question I posed to the respondents. Their replies yielded at least four

---

[1]It is possible that other studies of former nuns, based on larger samples, may find that type of pathway chosen is related to these variables. At present, no data exist to support these hypothesized relationships.

reasons for choosing a leave over the dispensation and suggests the varied functions served by this pathway.

First, a leave of absence was a way to reduce the trauma of giving up a major role and life-style. Such relinquishments are personally and socially trying on an individual whose identity, relations, and predictable round of experiences is embedded in a certain social location. Some respondents were acutely aware of the fact that, "in making a break with a passage or ending it, the letdown is almost sure to come" (Glaser & Strauss, 1971, p. 50). One former nun put it this way in response to my inquiry:

> (If you were certain that you didn't want to return why did you ask for a leave instead of a dispensation?) It wasn't so final. It's easier on you to get a leave because it helps to make the transition gradually. It's probably a security thing in a way, feeling that it's not the complete end of everything. It helps to ease you out.

For some, then, a leave worked to cushion the immediacy and the shock of role relinquishment, gently "easing" the person out of her role.

While a dispensation was permanent and made reentry into religious life extremely difficult, a leave was a temporary suspension of one's role. In this sense, the leave also served a second purpose; namely, it was used as a side bet in case the secular world did not meet the woman's expectation or she found she could not make the passage work. Two women point out this use of the leave by noting that:

> If you have a leave of absence, I felt if I really was unhappy out I could always come back whereas if I had asked for a dispensation that was it! It's not the final, final decision. You still can come back if you want to.
> * * * * * *
> A dispensation was too final. What if I didn't like it out there? What if I really couldn't adjust? With a leave I could come back, but not with a dispensation. I knew I could make it (in the lay world) but what if I was wrong?

The sense of finality posed by a dispensation made this the most frequent of the four reasons for choosing the leave of absence. It gave the nun the greatest option and control over her passage. She knew this and deliberately selected what, for her, seemed the most efficacious mode of exit.

A third function of the leave centered on it as a more "socially acceptable" way of exiting, less likely to arouse the disapproval of one's superiors:

> It would ease me out a little slower by asking for a leave and I think for the community too—like it was less drastic to ask Mother for a leave. Well, like it would be easier to ask your parents to get engaged than to ask to get married.

This quote, in fact, not only underscores the greater social approval given to requests for a leave; it also reveals that the leave served more than one function for each nun. Perhaps the analogy of parental approval for marriage is also subconsciously indicative of the adolescent posture commented on earlier.

The fourth reason expressed for choosing a leave was mentioned by only about one-third of the sample and, interestingly, was the official purpose of a leave, "to think things through, to put things in perspective, to figure out what I really wanted." In recalling the order's official and intended purpose in granting a leave we should note that neither of the first three uses of the leave was chosen for its formal purpose. The order had only one thing in mind in granting leaves of absence, the nuns others in requesting them. We are obviously not talking about duplicity here but rather about the multiple uses of meanings and purposes that informally arise in social action. For each woman the choice of a leave amounted to the development of a strategy that she believed provided the best route out of religious life.

The requests for a leave of absence can also be seen as a measure of the difficulty most persons have in leaving major roles and ways of life. It demonstrates a desire by them to smooth the exit and leave open options for returning. We can find analogous functions in the predivorce separation, the trial marriage, and the "matriculation continued" year off from college. Modes of relinquishment, then, can be made, even in emergent passages, in ways that decrease the costs of leaving, provide greater control over the passage, and buttress the emotional strain of a complete and swift break with social roles.

At this point I want to introduce the second dimension of role relinquishment being considered in this chapter. In addition to choosing among *alternate routes* away from a role, relinquishment also involves the *timing* of such departures. When to leave a role is as important a question as how to leave and leads us to consider how these women developed strategies for timing their exit from religious life.

In institutionalized passages, guidelines, benchmarks, and strategies have been developed to tell us when to leave certain roles in order to enter others. These temporal expectations serve to relieve most of us—as workers, citizens, students, spouses—of the burden of making such critical decisions. For instance, schooling officially begins at age five or six, childbearing years are expected to be between the ages of twenty and forty, a proper amount of time is expected to elapse between the death of one's spouse and the resumption of an active social life. Through laws, customs, and rituals we are moved through role passages on various societal timetables. Further, these more institutionalized temporal strategies facilitate social order by keeping aggregates of people moving at approximately the same time through the different sectors and stages of social life. Thus, most students enter college immediately after high school, most people first marry in their early twenties, or retire in their sixties. By way of contrast emergent passages have few such temporal guidelines and their absence raises intriguing sociological problems.

The person-in-transit through an emergent passage has to create the proper timing for leaving a role. But how does one come to sense the right time to leave? Which cues to pay attention to? Which piece of advice to listen to? Which factors to weigh?

In exploring these questions with respondents it became clear that the women considered this problem of timing to be of considerable importance, second only to having made the decision to leave. One factor that came into play in choosing an effective strategy for leaving was the practical consideration of employment. Since this was a teaching order and all respondents were primarily educators, they knew that teaching positions were not likely to be available until the end of the academic year. According to one former nun, "I felt I would have a better chance of getting a teaching position for next year so I stayed for four months longer." This assessment of the availability of teaching positions, for which they felt most qualified, was one of the reasons that the majority of them left in June. This was true even for those who had already decided to reconsider their commitment to religious life and had requested permission to do so from the order. The desire to remain until June was also made for altruistic reasons. By delaying the exit the nun tried to minimize the order's cost in losing a member without much opportunity to get a replacement for her:

> I finally made up my mind to leave about November and yet, as I told Mother, I wanted to stay the rest of that year because I felt I owed it to them so they wouldn't have to get a teacher. (Owed it to whom?) To the Motherhouse, the community.

Another event that influenced timing was the leave-taking of other nuns. Throughout the interviews respondents stressed the fact that their friends in religious life provided much of the encouragement, strength, and support they needed during the most difficult time of coming to decide whether or not to leave. Once their friends began to leave, however, respondents expressed increased anxiety, loneliness, and doubt about the possibility of remaining much longer in the community. Many nuns left sooner than they would have because their major source of social support was declining. To some extent the fact that others were leaving also diminished one's commitment to stay and thus affected not only timing but also motivation. In their own words, five former nuns discuss the impact their friends leaving had on them:

> All of these people are leaving. My friends. I was one of the last to go. This had a big affect on me. (In what way?) I though that I didn't want to be the last rat on a sinking ship. They were leaving and I felt that if people like this are going— people who I felt really believed in what I did, and wanted the same things—then what am I hanging in for? Am I going to wait until I'm forty?
> * * * * * *
> My whole view of what religious life should be was so different from those who were staying and so, although I told Mother in May that I would stay for

another year because I was Assistant Principal of the school, within that week I knew I couldn't do it. I couldn't stay with those who differed so much from my philosophy.

* * * * * *

It was easier to leave when I did because everyone else was leaving or had already left. As others left it also paved the way for those who wanted to.

* * * * * *

I'm sure I would have stayed at least another year or so if my friends—those I believed in—had not left. When they went there was nothing there; and I left that June.

* * * * * *

I can remember, we would sit down—we had a book with all the names of the people in the community—and we kept crossing them off as they left. We just put a line through as they left. I saw the people who were staying and decided I couldn't stay for another year. I didn't have enough support. Everybody who thought like me was leaving.

To borrow a phrase, respondents came to time their leaving while the "reversing is good" (Glaser & Strauss, 1971, p. 30). They evaluated the impact of the others' leave-taking and timed their exit accordingly. This may partially explain the somewhat epidemic rash of nuns who left the convent over a few short years. Role relinquishments may have a contagious effect and may themselves be a source of mass exits from social roles. The exodus of many groups in the last decade from their conventional roles as citizens, women, and students, for instance, may be understood as partially a function of this contagion. This is to say, the relinquishment by some may hasten that of others by providing an example of a feasible alternative, by confronting others with the need for taking action and making a choice, and by leaving a social vacuum within which others are not willing to function.

Temporal strategies also were bound up in estimates of psychological readiness. Respondents made assessments of their feelings of emotional preparation for leaving and carefully compared themselves to others who had left in terms of this readiness. They were aware of what can be called "premature exits" by some nuns who were not yet ready, emotionally and mentally, to face relinquishment:

> I almost had talked myself into leaving before that year. From September to January I had thought about leaving and I believe that if I had left then, instead of in June, it would have been a much more traumatic adjustment for me to have made. (Why?) I don't think I was prepared to leave at that point. (In what way?) As far as adjustment. (Could you explain that?) I was upset because I had left my friends through a transfer to a different house. I was bitter. I needed more time to work things out. (What did staying that extra year do for you?) It made me a much stronger person, as far as my own beliefs, and there was no remorse when I left. Had I left earlier I would have thought to myself that I had left because I was hurt.

Phrases such as, "I didn't feel I was ready to leave then," or "I had psyched myself up" enough to leave, or "She left before she really had decided to leave" were extremely frequent during this phase of the interview. They underscore the importance of temporal calculations in emergent passages and the ad hoc nature of these strategies. Additionally, the data highlight the existence of poorly timed exits—leaving a role too early or waiting too long before leaving. In both cases temporal miscalculations can be become problematic during subsequent parts of a passage. Teenagers who leave adolescence too early to cope with the demands of marriage and movie stars or professional athletes who wait too long to step down, immediately come to mind as instances of the possible consequences of temporal miscalculation. The difficulty in formulating a sense of confidence in the optimum timing of role relinquishment, by persons going through less formalized passages, forces us to appreciate this taken-for-granted part of most social life.

As we close this part of the book we should briefly recall the relinquishment of religious life as a phase shaped by the interplay of personal and social factors. Analyses of the decision to leave, the rehearsals for secular life, and the creation of strategies for leaving reveal a social being who grapples with the demands of an amorphous role phase. Our discussion of relinquishment ends at this point, with a reminder that formally this phase terminates with a nun's request for final dispensation from her vows. Yet, as we have seen, for the majority of the women relinquishment actually had occurred prior to this formal request. These respondents, even though only on leaves of absence, knew they were very unlikely to return to religious life. For the others, they would remain tied to their role as nuns, emotionally and behaviorally, even after requesting final dispensation. It is obvious, then, that while we can utilize formal measures of role exit as one index of relinquishment these are not sufficient benchmarks for distinguishing among the stages of a passage.

How, then, are we to know when certain phases of a passage are over? How can we speak of a person's successful movement to new stages? Specifically, when do women begin to live not as nuns but as other kinds of people, lay people playing secular roles? I raise this question now because in Part III of this book I want to examine the transitional phase of this passage as former nuns begin their foray into secular society. We immediately become concerned with their successful transition to secular life; that is, their accommodation to lay roles.

I have purposefully avoided using the value-laden term "adjustment" when speaking of accomplishing the passage to secular life. The term carries with it the assumption that persons must adjust to given roles and life-styles and that we, as sociologists, can decide the extent to which this adjustment has occurred. However, from a sociological perspective it is clear that all role passages, to different degrees, entail both personal and interactional problems to which some kind of adjustment or accommodation must be made. I propose in this study to use the term adjustment as conceptualized by Goode (1956) in his study of the postdivorce adjustment process. His definition avoids a psychological reduction of the term adjustment while capturing the personal and social accommodations that surround a passage between roles. Goode (1956) defines the process of adjustment as one:

> by which *a disruption of role sets and patterns, and of existing social relations, is incorporated into the individual's life pattern such that the roles accepted and assigned do not take the prior divorce into account as the primary point of reference:* In more commonsense terms, the woman is no longer "ex-wife," or "divorcee" primarily, but first of all "co-worker," "date," or "bride." (p. 19)

In applying this definition to our study, we would substitute the words "convent experience" for "the prior divorce" and "ex-nun" for "ex-wife." This definition of adjustment, then, focuses on the degree to which our respondents have integrated the convent experience into their total life situation in such a way that they live "by daily and future demands" of their new social locations "rather than by constant reference to the ties defined by" their experiences in religious life. This conceptualization sensitizes us to treat adjustment as a personal and social phenomenon. On the personal, social-psychological level adjustment entails alterations in self-imagery and social identity. Does the respondent retain a definition of herself as an "ex-nun" or does she come to see herself as reflected in present or future roles? On the interpersonal, sociological level we must also ask if *others* define and respond to her in terms of her past religious role or according to present role assignations? Our definition of a successful passage between religious and secular roles can now be specified: to the extent that former nuns come to define themselves in terms of present and future roles such as employees, women, homeowners, dating partners, or citizens; and, to the extent that they and others base their mutual relations not on past convent identities and roles but on ongoing ones, we can speak of them as making a successful passage to secular life.

In the next part of the book, in Chapter 6 I will examine the respondent's transition to the intimate sectors of social life: friendship, love, and sexuality; in Chapter 7 I will discuss the respondent's resumption of her roles as woman, worker, and social adult; and Chapter 8 will contain a theoretical overview of this transitional phase of the passage.

PART III
THE TRANSITIONAL PHASE

6

Entering the Spheres of Intimacy: Love, Sexuality, and Friendship

PRELUDE TO SECULAR LIFE

With the convent behind them the former nuns entered a transitional phase of improvisation, learning, and evaluation. Unlike those moving in a more institutionalized role transition, with its tried and known rules, customs, and standards for assessment, these women were moving through a phase that they would have to shape on their own. Their location at a social frontier was illustrated by the tentative and general aspirations they held at the time of relinquishment. They spoke of "just wanting to lead a normal life," "getting settled and taking things as they come," "hanging loose and enjoying myself," "getting a job and meeting new people." Beyond arrangements for the practical necessities of residence and job, they had formulated few advance plans, timetables, or strategies and initially made ad hoc responses to events and situations as they arose. In one sense, these loosely formulated expectations minimized the potential negative impact of uniformed choices, improper timings, premature hopes, and unforseen delays that inevitably are part of emergent transitions.

What were those first days and weeks of "being out" like? Respondents remembered that early stage as one of great release, heady pleasures, and emotional exhilaration. For a short time they enjoyed the mental tranquility that comes from having made a decision, and the rush of pleasure that surrounds newly resumed experiences. Respondents recalled "how great it was" to sleep until late in the morning, to just get in a car and go "without having to ask permission," to stay up for nights on end watching the talk shows and movies, to eat when and what they pleased, to not have a scheduled routine or need to consider another's wishes before acting. Their days were spent renewing family ties, resting, shopping, and visiting friends. They characterized them as "exciting," "crazy," "new," "free," "fun," "peaceful," and "terrific."

Depending on their motives for leaving religious life, respondents had somewhat distinct reactions to their first weeks in secular society. Those who were "pulled" out of the convent by the promise of secular rewards were more active during this time in making social contacts, establishing their new residence, looking for a job, and so forth. For those who left for ideological reasons, who felt "pushed" out of the convent, it was a time of social delay. They declared a moratorium on specific decisions, strategies, and plans of action in an attempt to consolidate their emotional and social situation. Now less burdened by the emotional strain of having made a decision, they attempted to bring their past into sharper focus, to reexamine their decision to leave, and to evaluate the cause and meanings of such a decision. They were more likely than those who left for personal reasons to devote the earliest phases of their leave of absence to the intended purpose of the leave— reevaluating their commitment to religious life.

This early expressive stage, lasting about six weeks, was replaced by a more instrumental, practical one for virtually all respondents. One woman describes the situation vividly:

> At first it was just great fun being out. I relaxed, slept, read the papers, went down the shore, stayed up late, thought about things; but that couldn't go on for too long. It just wasn't real and the newness began to wear off.

These former nuns, after a few weeks had passed, began to make fuller accommodations to residence, family, job, and citizenship.

Conceptually, we can introduce our discussion of these accommodations by distinguishing two different tasks confronting our respondents. As we suggested earlier, these women had not moved along with their age peers through the "typical" sequence of roles associated with both their sex and their age roles. To a lesser extent they also lagged behind in sectors of occupational, economic, and general social life. Glaser and Strauss (1971, p. 31) term this phenomenon an "arrested passage." Specifically, former nuns found themselves to be "behind" in age and sex-role performances, lacking much of the achievements, self-awareness, experience, knowledge, exposures, and skills conventionally expected of *adult women*. How they handle the attendant problems of this age deviance will be one of the major themes of this part of the book. The issues of age deviance and arrested passage are, we should note, common problems confronting many persons who leave total institutions. These problems underscore the fact that role playing, like other skills, requires sufficient practice and polishing to maintain effectiveness. It is not an automatic, built-in propensity to behave and feel in certain ways.

In order to bridge these gaps resulting from being in religious life, the respondents had to devise strategies to accomplish three tasks. First, they had to discover what the general expectations for women at their age were; how women were percieved by others; what others would assume or expect of them; and what might be taken for granted in everyday situations. Second, they had to seek out people who could serve as informants and evaluators of their progress in "catching up" with their peers. These socializing agents would serve as sources of knowledge, criticism, and validation for the former nun. Finally, to the degree that respondents wanted to avoid revealing their past, they had to go about the above activities in a circumspect manner. These women suspected that negative sanctions, embarrassment, and "explanations" might well follow the disclosure of their former life as nuns. Thus, while they were attempting to gain the knowledge of social expectations for their age and sex roles, and to solicit validators of their progress in "catching up," they also had to try to appear *au courant;* they had to present themselves as "normal" persons, at ease with themselves and their secular roles, lest they "give their past away." Many people returning from total institutions— POWs, criminals, the mentally ill, orphans—face similar challenges in picking up arrested passages and share, with former nuns, the need to devise ways of meeting these social exigencies. In addition to the problem of picking up arrested passages, respondents were also confronted with a second one of managing multiple role changes, such as setting priorities and seeking supportive links between different roles. This topic will be discussed separately in Part IV of the book.

Although many respondents had begun to anticipate the role changes they would confront once they left religious life, and some had actually activated segments of certain roles before leaving, it was in this transitional phase that more extensive learning and experimentation took place. They were now in secular society, on their own, having to make their way through the institutional and role complex that characterizes "normal" life. We are now ready to begin our exploration of their initial exposure to love, sexuality, and friendship.

LOVE AND SEXUALITY

In our society, individuals are expected to begin initial involvements in intimate relations during adolescence (Chafetz, 1974; Erikson, 1968) and, by early adulthood, to have developed satisfying emotional and sexual relationships. It is beyond the scope of this book to chronicle the changing meanings of love and sexuality that have been developed in American society over the past decade or so. The reemergence of the feminist movement in the late sixties and the publication of the iconoclastic study of *Human Sexual Response* by Masters and Johnson (1966) generated a series of debates over the nature of human sexuality, love, and the roles of women and men that continues unabated.

In the popular literature, feminist novelists, poets, and theoreticians have opposed traditional understandings of female sexuality and women's roles in the expressive spheres of love, marriage, and family. Betty Friedan, Jill Johnston, Kate Millet, Germaine Greer, Warren Farrell, and Gail Sheehy have become well-known critics of established views on intimate relations. In academic circles, Masters and Johnson brought sexual behavior into the laboratory for examination and emerged with a set of startling, and hotly contested findings, perhaps the most significant of which centered on the importance of the clitoris for female orgasm. Although their work contributed to a methodological breakthrough in the scientific approach toward studying sexual behavior it ignored the *social context* in which sexual behavior is learned and derives its meaning for human beings. This gap has begun to be filled by social scientists who, beginning with Gagnon and Simon (1973), have stressed the importance of social, rather than solely biological, factors in our development of sexual identities and our behavior as sexual beings. Feminist scholars in particular (Chafetz, 1974; Laws & Schwartz, 1977; Safilios-Rothschild, 1977) are involved in critical analyses of even these social perspectives on sexuality insofar as they, too, fail "to transcend the limitations of traditional thinking about women" (Laws & Schwartz, 1977, p. viii). The discussion of how former nuns came to activate their sexual identity in the lay world and their resumption of intimate relationships as women is grounded in my own social and feminist perspectives on these issues.

Of special interest in this study are two concepts which highlight the exigencies of a former nun's passage to intimate roles. The first, sexual identity, is a concept which refers to an individual's "awareness of herself as a female and of the attributes that make up her femaleness" (Laws & Schwartz, 1977, p. 22). This identity is learned rather than innate and it is grounded in the social meanings we give to biological attributes as well as in the cultural definitions of what it means to be a woman or a man. On this personal level, sexual identity is organized around such questions as what does it mean for me that I am a woman? How should I, as a woman, respond to myself and others? What kind of a woman am I and can I become?

The second concept, sexual scripts, was introduced by Gagnon and Simon (1973) and calls attention to the social level of sexuality. Sexual scripts are the accumulated acts and roles developed to govern the sexual area of social life. Like scripts for plays, these and other social scripts define the rules, meanings, and sanctions that are appropriate to social life. As social actors we play roles according to provided scripts, rehearsing our parts, being coached, trying to carefully follow our scripts. In their book, *Sexual Scripts* (1977), Laws and Schwartz examine the issue of female sexuality in light of the available and changing sexual scripts for women. According to Reiss (1960) our society has, at different times and for different groups, made available various sexual scripts. The single standard of abstinence, which allows sexual intercourse only between spouses, is still the preferred and official one, although the double standard which provides greater sexual freedom for the male has come to be generally accepted as a sexual script. Emerging in the sixties was a new script, permissiveness with affection, which "holds that coitus is acceptable for both sexes when the partners are in love" (Laws & Schwartz, 1977, p. 48). This script, also referred to as "the sexual revolution of the sixties" is similar to the other two in that love is tied to sex, heterosexuality, and marriage. A fourth script, permissiveness without affection, permits sex without justifications of affection and entails no necessary connection between sex and marriage, love, or monogamy. This script, argue some, may be gaining in popularity in certain sectors of the society (Laws & Schwartz, 1977, p. 54).

All of these scripts open up a wide range of choices for both sexes; for example, we can choose among various sexual preferences, we can select monogamy with or without marriage, we can have "open" or "closed" relationships and so forth. The choices among scripts obviously have an impact on our sexual identity as well for this identity is developed through and tied to sexual scripts. Thus, for all of us in pluralistic America, a sexual identity is problematic (Laws & Schwartz, 1977, p. 12) and even more so for women whose scripts have for so long been socially constructed by and for men.

For the women leaving religious life sexual identity and sexual scripts were even more problematic. The overwhelming majority of nuns, first of all, enter religious life immediately after high school; in our sample this was true with one exception. One can hardly expect high school girls to have accumulated the experiences necessary for a solid base of emotional and sexual activity. In addition, once a high school girl had decided to enter the convent she was even less likely than her age peers to pursue the usual round of adolescent dating and intimacy. Once in the convent, of course, intimate relations were prohibited and contact with males strictly prescribed. In fact, such was the radical resocialization of intimacy that even close relationship between nuns was forbidden. "Particular friendships," as they were called, were cause for negative sanctions and steps were taken to break up these relationships. Further, all but four of the respondents had entered the convent before the sexual revolution of the sixties took hold and were socialized to the more conservative sexual scripts of the forties and fifties. In sum, then, the former nun emerges in secular society with minimal experience in dating, sex, and romantic love. During most of her time in religious life her sexual identity as a woman was put aside, as was her sexual behavior. In a sense, she was also not fully conscious of the changing sexual scripts available in the lay world since they were not salient to her as a celibate woman. How did these women experience their transition to active sexual identities and intimate roles?

Let us first consider the six respondents who were either engaged or married at the time of the interview. Even today, the sexual script that ties together sex, romantic love, heterosexuality, and marriage is the ideal pattern (Laws & Schwartz, 1977, p. 54) and our respondents accepted this script as most valid for them also. The former nun who was engaged or married was considered, by most respondents, to "have made it" back to secular life. They were defined, through engagement and marriage to men, to have successfully scaled the most difficult and final step in full immersion to lay life.

The engaged or married respondent did not differ from the single respondent in terms of number of years in religious life, length of time in secular society, or type of vow taken. In fact, even the respondent's earlier comments of the presumed advantage of age for finding a spouse did not hold true; the fact that proportionately as many respondents over thirty-five as under were engaged or married suggests that age itself was not a major factor. One pattern, however, seemed clear. All but one of the respondents was engaged to or married a man with whom she was romantically involved or knew well while she was still in the convent. This finding lends support to our earlier hypothesis that rehearsals tend to enhance one's ability to play new roles. These early romantic, sexual, or emotional relations by respondents while still in the convent dramatically reduced the need to learn sexual scripts and become proficient at playing them.[1]

In effect, these six women short-circuited the process of negotiating a sexual and love passage by moving into an already established intimate relation. They thus avoided many of the problems surrounding the ubiquitous search for the proper mate. Nor did they grapple much with questions of sexual identity or choices among alternative sexual scripts. In fact, in my interviews with them I was surprised by the relative absence of doubt, anxiety, learning, and improvisation that did arise in the interviews with former nuns who were single women at the time they were interviewed This is not to say of course, that no learning, accommodation, and choice was involved in getting engaged or married; however, these matters were mainly personal and idiosyncratic and do not highlight the issues of sexual identity and script. We turn our attention then to those former nuns who were still single at the time of the interview because the transistion to intimacy is better illustrated by looking at those who, to borrow an old refrain, "made all the stops along the way."

---

[1] In questioning respondents about their intimate relations both during and after their convent experience I inquired about their possible relations with both women and men. No respondent indicated she had been intimately involved with a woman. However, four respondents indicated they knew other nuns and former nuns who had romantic or sexual relations with women at some stage in the overall passage. One respondent stated she wished I had not raised the question because "many people think we're lesbians, all of us living so close together like that."

Developing confidence in one's identity as a woman and in one's ability to play out a particular sexual script depends on many factors. Some of these include becoming aware of "the rules of the game" in the sense of knowing the rituals, codes, and sanctions that govern the spheres of love and sex; planning or finding opportunities to meet willing partners; controlling personal appearance and other modes of impression management (Goffman, 1959); and pacing oneself through various stages of intimate involvement and disengagement.

It is in discussing their early dating experiences that we find evidence of how much these women had to learn and get used to. Men were then still relational strangers and respondents frequently referred to "having to get used to being with" men, feeling "ill at ease" in their company, not sure of "how men think," and concerned about "how a man would react" to them. Of course, the roles scripted for men and women had been changing while they were in the convent, especially with regard to the appearance of the permissiveness with affection option during the sixties. One respondent, a twenty-six-year-old woman, who had only been a nun for six years, remarked on these changes:

> I had not been in that long but I realized soon after I left that men, and women too, were a lot more aggressive than when I was in the dating scene. The rules had changed. When you went away for a weekend it was now expected that you would sleep with him. I had to kind of grow into that gradually. I really did. It was a surprise to me.

Two other women, who were in religious life for approximately a decade, reflected on other changes in sexual scripts:

> I had to learn to recognize the lines guys would hand you. It was no longer "if you love me prove it" but now that you were "uptight" or "hung-up" if you wouldn't play ball. All the cliches—how you're supposed to act, the signals that are sent back and forth across the bar—I'm not sure I even know them now.
> * * * * * *
> I'd go to a dance and would be terrified that somebody would ask me to dance. Not having danced in twelve years meant you were still in the frame of mind when men and women danced holding each other. I would watch the people moving around, trying to get some idea of what they were doing.

The process of learning about expected behavior for both sexes and the folkways, skills, and postures of the dating scene was a variegated one, each woman selecting sources of information in different ways. One woman, for example, solicited from her female friend strategies for rejecting the unwanted interest of a male acquaintance—the classic "brush-off" had to be learned anew. Another respondent asked her brother to give her "a man's opinion on the new sexual morality." Some women carefully watched men "when they weren't looking," to eavesdrop on conversational and gestural cues to relations between the sexes. Laughing as she recalled it, another woman recalled "This friend of mine who keeps the books on new sex techniques coming in. She gave me *The Sensuous Woman, The Happy Hooker, All You Wanted To Know About Sex.*" On their jobs, respondents' female work colleagues would inadvertently provide opinions and guidelines for former nuns as they discussed their own private lives during lunch and after work hours:

> I would listen to them talking about their affairs and who was on the pill, and what her doctor said, and how another one was ditching somebody, and you just pick up ideas like that too.

Thus, in any number of ways these women were serving as their own socializing agents, seeking knowledge and cues of extant sexual scripts.

Their absence from secular social life and the emerging changes in sexual identities and rules for behavior is clearly evidenced when they discussd what, for most of them, was mentioned as the most difficult problem in this area: "finding places to meet men." Their place of employment reportedly provided few chances to meet men because most of their male colleagues were married and therefore not eligible in their eyes. In the beginning stages of employment, at least, respondents also noted that they had not yet made friends with women "who have a friend I'd like you to meet." Their unwillingness to date married men and their desired reliance on female friends to provide a social introduction perhaps reflects the more traditional socialization they were acting upon.

If that is the case, one would expect that the more acceptable places for mate selection developing in the sixties and early seventies would meet with resistance and this, indeed, proved to be true. Most respondents reacted negatively to singles bars, singles weekends, and other such gatherings of the unattached in urban areas. There were a few exceptions, however, among those former nuns who, as young adults before becoming nuns, frequented bars and social clubs at summer resorts or in their local community. They were not hesitant to go to these places now, as others were, but nevertheless they too found it difficult to find promising dating partners. This difficulty is not only an expression of their experiential unfamiliarity with intimacy but also a consequence of the changing scripts for sexuality. In different ways, four women underscore this theme:

> It was very hard for me at first to meet eligible men that I found attractive. I was very self-conscious. I didn't know how to talk to men—witty remarks and those things. If I went to a bar, I was very nervous and I felt that I was being very obvious. I just didn't like the whole scene. If a man sat next to me I wouldn't know what to say to start a conversation or if he was too forward I would be

turned off. I only went to a singles bar a few times. I just don't like the atmosphere really and don't feel comfortable there.

＊ ＊ ＊ ＊ ＊

You know, the world I left in 1955 and what I see now in these cocktail lounges is totally different and there's lots of things I'm not familiar with. (Could you give some examples?) Like the guys just assuming you're an easy make, putting hands over you, being wise. Who needs it? I don't like those kind of men and yet where do you go? The singles bars with married men who are all too willing to date you.

＊ ＊ ＊ ＊ ＊

I remember the first and last time I went to a bar. It was devastating! The loud music, the smoke, the crowds—like you were really almost on parade. I was afraid. (Of what?) What do you talk about? How do you talk? I didn't dance so I suppose I've just given up on places like that—it's not for me.

＊ ＊ ＊ ＊ ＊

When I was a teenager only "bad girls" went to bars and lounges—it just wasn't the thing for college-type girls. Now, of course, that's changed but I still find that feeling inside me.

The most acceptable type of organized opportunity to socialize was the singles club, which involves a variety of structured activities ranging from dances, parties, and lectures to theater trips and ski weekends. Respondents would occasionally go to some of the dances, always with a former nun, and at times they would be successful in dating someone they met there. As these women became more adept at social skills, comfortable with their jobs, financially secure and more confident as women (all of which will be discussed in later sections of the book) the problems of "finding eligible men" lessened in importance. Of the fourteen respondents who were single when interviewed about half were dating at least on occasion. In fact, dating activity (as opposed to marriage) did differ markedly by the respondent's age. Those in their late twenties and early thirties were likely to have had their first date three to six months after leaving the convent while for older respondents it usually took nine months to a year after leaving before having first dated. The younger respondents were also more likely to be dating about once a month while the older ones averaged a date once every six months or so. Even though there were too few cases to make a firm comparison this relation between age and dating seemed to hold true even when length of time out in secular life was held constant.

The remainder of this section will concentrate on four aspects of the transition to intimate relations, each one capable of being viewed as a vehicle for enhancing one's sexual identity and easing the transition to romantic and sexual roles.

The first aspect centers around the respondent's evaluation of men in general and their male dating partners in particular. I was somewhat surprised at the considerably positive view they held of men, especially in light of the emerging feminist consciousness, at its peak in the early seventies, which underscored the more negative dimensions of masculinity and male sexuality. These women were aware of the feminist movement, many of them had read such feminist works as *The Feminine Mystique* and *Sexual Politics* and even debated such issues as the sexual objectification of women. Yet, they frequently alluded to the fact that they were "fortunate" in having encountered primarily "gentle," "kind," "considerate," and "understanding" men. Those other men, "who tried to get smart" or "only wanted to go to bed," or treated you like a sex object" were seen as the rare exception. While some might argue that their response only confirms the distorted exaggerations of feminism, others, with equal facility, might wonder where these men have been hiding! My own interpretation of the data leads me to suggest that these respondents were highly *selective* in pursuing and accepting male companionship. By avoiding the singles bar, singles retreat, married men, and casual "pickup" they in effect limited their pool of potential dating and sex partners to those who more likely matched their own preferences and values. Their selectivity, then, was one way they controlled the unwanted aspects of romantic and sexual initiation and partially explains the overwhelming favorable experiences they reported regarding men. One respondent's remarks nicely illustrate this mechanism:

> I didn't just go out with anybody, a stranger or some guy who tried to pick me up. I wasn't that desperate. I got to know him first and only then decided if I wanted to date him.

While selection was one way of negotiating favorable intimacy a second strategy was to inform her date that she was once a nun:

> (When did you tell him you had been in the convent?) It was after we had been out twice and before he ever kissed me. (Why did you tell him?) I'm really not sure. I think I was very self-conscious about my lack of experience sexually and yet I didn't want him to think something was wrong with me—that I was weird or anything. So maybe I told him because I would make more sense to him once he knew.

A number of respondents also reported this same event and it suggests that disclosing themselves as former nuns, whether intentionally or unwittingly, signaled to their male partner the woman's lack of intimate experience. This disclosure, in turn, then cues the man as to what should be his appropriate range of expectation and behavior vis-a-vis his date. By making reference to one's past role the former nun can "account" (Scott & Lyman, 1963) for a present failure in expected role performance. As Laws and Schwartz (1977, p. 69) note a sexual script is divided into age-graded stages so that women at different stages are expected to have accumulated a certain repertoire of sexual experience. Accounts, then, also assuage suspicion as to one's normalcy and help smooth over difficulties in romantic and sexual exchanges.

A third aspect of the transition to intimate relations has to do with the respondents' shift in orientation toward sexual activity. All respondents, but especially those with little or no prior sexual experience, were quite concerned about their presentation of sexual selves. The problem was not primarily that they doubted their ability to respond to others physically. Rather, they expressed concern over their ability to engage in sexual interactions with ease and grace. They were confronted, for perhaps the first time, with real opportunities to evaluate their personal sexual mores and their accepted definitions of love. They also wanted very much to be responded to as women, seeking social validation from men that they indeed were women. And, ultimately, they were aware, as most women are, of the importance of sex and sexual attitudes in the presentation of women as sexual beings. As Safilios-Rothschild (1977) observes, "Women, forced to attract men since only through them could they get a 'piece of the pie,' have had to become sex objects... because sexuality is the only 'hot' and desirable commodity over which women have exclusive rights" (p. 36).

What kinds of sexual attitudes did respondents bring to their transitional phase and why, in an effort to validate themselves as women and assure an active social life, did these attitudes change? All respondents at first presented what would be considered traditional attitudes toward sexual activity (Safilios-Rothschild, 1977, p. 23). By that we mean that sexual activity is legitimized and valued when it is coupled with love, affection, and permanent commitment. An example of this orientation is provided by one younger woman:

> I don't want to have sexual relations with a man unless we mean something to each other in a special way; there has to be love there. I don't buy this idea of going to bed with a guy who you may not see after a few weeks. I'm looking for something permanent.

Respondents could be said to have emerged into secular society ready to follow the more traditional sexual scripts which tie love with sexuality and stress monogamy leading to future marriage (Laws & Schwartz, 1977, pp. 49–50). Respondents over thirty-five were more likely than younger ones to hold to the abstinence or double-standard scripts but generally all of them embraced the traditional standards of sexual morality.

A few respondents, primarily those who married within one to two years after leaving, retained this traditional sexual posture but more of them began to embrace a more "liberal" sexual orientation. The term liberal is put in quotes for special reasons. To some extent, separating love from sex is regarded in certain circles as a liberating script for women. It entails freedom for women to be sexual beings without the trappings of love, marriage, and permanence. For others, separating love from sex merely reduces women's script to that of men's and dehumanizes both sexes (Safilios-Rothschild, 1977, pp. 54–58). While I leave the reader to her or his own interpretation of the implication of such a separation, I want to stress the way in which changing attitudes toward sex served to meet the respondent's need to shape her transition into sexual intimacy. Specifically, some women engaged in sexual relations to deliberately affirm their femininity and womanhood.

> Probably what prompted this sexual relationship was a strong need I had to convince myself that I was a woman—that I was attractive to men. I felt I had to get involved in order to show myself that I was really like any other woman.

This comment reflects the traditional need to solicit male validation of one's role as a woman but, at the same time, reflects a departure from the traditional romantic justification for sex. Other women consciously became involved in sexual relations for the instrumental purposes of gaining sexual expertise:

> To tell you the truth, I viewed this affair as a learning experience. Maybe that's why I chose a married man. He was gentle, he was experienced. He taught me lots of things I didn't know. I owe much of my confidence to him.

Again, here is a theme reminiscent of traditional emphases on male sexual initiation of naive women but, as in the other quote, these comments also reflect deliberate attempts by respondents to manage their transition. It was partially as a by-product of these sexual relations, with or without emotional involvement, that respondents embraced different sexual scripts, gained confidence in their ability to be intimate, and developed a firmer sense of the female role.

Finally, the data yields a fourth dimension for handling sexual identity and sexual scripts—the change in the respondent's reference groups and role models. As the weeks and months in secular life passed, these women began to acquire new, lay friends; they worked alongside women at different stages of the life cycle; they encountered more directly the elaboration of the feminist movement—in these and other corners of social life they confronted emerging notions of sexual alternatives and modes of intimate relations. One woman speaks about the impact of her job:

> When I first came to work here I had these prudish ideas about sex and I would talk with the girls at work and they were living what I considered wild lives— they went to bed with men they weren't engaged to, they dated divorced and married men, they took the pill, they went on weekends together, you know, the whole scene. As I got to be friends with them I began to realize that they weren't that different from me. They were good at their jobs; they were kind; they were intelligent; and I began to think that maybe my ideas about sex were old fashioned; you didn't have to be a terrible person to do these things.

Another woman considers the effects of just "being in the world":

> If anyone had ever told me that in two years I would be seeing a married man, I would have said they were crazy. It's funny how your values change, but after being in the world, meeting other types of people with different standards you

come to evaluate that old morality which I didn't have a chance to test and to realize that there are other approaches than the one you held.

The effects of the feminist movement are recalled by another respondent:

When I first left the convent, I thought that women's lib was all wet. I wanted to be a woman and didn't want to apologize for it. After meeting some of these people, however, who criticize the role of women I have begun to rethink my own femininity, my sense of who I am as a woman and as a person.

The shift in reference groups, apparent in the above quotations, served to shape the respondent's identity as a woman, and engender a reevaluation of her standards for intimate relationships. These four themes—selection of sexual partners, "accounts" of one's past role as a nun, changes in sexual script, and shifts in reference groups—in their own way served to validate the respondent's identity as a woman, to accumulate a round of sexual expertise, and to facilitate the passage to intimate relations.

By way of summary, we recall that former nuns entered the secular society with a sexual identity and script that was acquired in early socialization and that, by and large, did not demand assessment or reconsideration as long as they were in religious life. These were identities and scripts that were not salient in the daily round of their lives as celibate nuns. When they reenter secular society, however, they begin to be exposed to experiences, persons, and situations that call for a reevaluation of these identities and scripts. To the extent that past standards impede the acquisition of presently valued roles they will be modified or abandoned. In the remaining part of this chapter we will examine the impact of friendship as an extension of the respondent's sphere of intimacy.

FRIENDSHIP

Unlike the transitional adjustments to love and sexual intimacy, establishing and maintaining bonds of friendship and sociability were not as difficult for the former nun. Although "particular friendhsips" were prohibited in religious life respondents did develop networks of friends and acquaintances while they were nuns. In fact, many of them developed strong emotional ties to other nuns and lay women and, to this extent, felt confident in their ability to embrace secular friendship roles.

The focus of our discussion of friendship, then, does not revolve around learning and acquiring new social roles. Rather, we want to examine the consequences of *different types of friendship networks* for the respondents' adjustment to secular life. Specifically, there were two types of friendship circles available to the former nun: one consisted of nuns and former nuns, women who had common role bonds with the respondent; the other consisted of lay women who did not know the respondent while she was in the convent.[2] Did respondents differ among themselves in terms of the type of friendship circle they maintained? Did the type change over time? What were the costs and rewards of retaining ties with friends from religious life or shifting one's circle to new friends? As we shall see, these two social circles contributed in different ways to both the success and difficulties of passing through this transitional phase.

Upon first leaving the convent *all* respondents reported as their closest friends both other former nuns or women who were still nuns. There was a greater tendency for younger respondents (under thirty-five) to name a lay person among their circle of close friends but they too were still primarily tied to other former nuns at first. However, the data reveal that changes in both the composition of the friendship network and its size occurred over time. Holding constant the length of time respondents had spent in the secular world we found that making lay friends was easier for younger respondents because their age peers were not that different from them in terms of life-course interests and experiences. The younger respondents stated that they found many single women their age in the social community and that, in time, they began to have more and more in common with them. For the older respondents the situation was different. Their secular peers were likely to be married and have a family; their friendship groups were more stable and more difficult to penetrate; their patterns of leisure, sociability, and neighboring were more settled; their social identity and vocational commitments more secure. Older respondents, in fact, were less likely to have lay persons as close friends or to have made new friends since they left the convent. Those respondents who had been in the lay world for longer periods of time were more likely than those recently out to name lay people as their closest friends. Also, the longer the respondent was in secular society the larger was her network of lay friends. Thus, the type of friends they had changed over time as did the size of their friendship network. We interpret this shift in their friends to be both a measure of their adjustment to secular society as well as the consequence of a conscious attempt by them to ease their passage to secular roles.

Let us examine this interpretation by exploring the ties respondents had with other former nuns. What was striking in their comments about friendships with other former nuns was the acute ambivalence they expressed. They were aware of the benefits of such ties and spoke with gratitude about them. Even before they had left the convent, many respondents were assisted in preparing for the exit by women who had left before them. As anticipatory

---

[2] We have deliberately chosen to focus only on female friendship in order to simplify the analysis. In addition, given the traditional difficulty of maintaining friendships between the sexes (Safilios-Rothschild, 1977) virtually all respondents spoke primarily of women friends.

socializing agents, their friends who went before them provided our respondents with information, social contacts, and practical suggestions. Two respondents recall this assistance:

> They helped you. They gave you ideas like how to go on an interview, or how to look for a job, or where to go; not to buy too many clothes in the beginning because your tastes change.
>
> * * * * * *
>
> Three of my friends who had left offered me their apartment and I stayed there until I could get myself together.

Beyond helping to prepare them for the contingencies of leaving, these friends were a source of much needed emotional support, especially during the respondents' first year in the lay world. When respondents felt depressed, confused, and anxious they could go to others who were likely to have experienced similar feelings and confronted similar problems. Because other former nuns were making the same passage to secular life they were able to provide the psychological support respondents required at different stages of their transition. These friends also helped respondents in assessing the meanings and strategies of coping with new social situations or picking up their arrested passages. The following quotations underscore the value of these functions:

> We'd get together and talk about our adjustments. How we were doing, what someone else was doing, and why it was good or bad. We'd talk about ways to meet people, how we handled different situations that would come up, the different problems that would arise or our feelings about what we were doing and where we were at.
>
> * * * * * *
>
> Probably nobody but another ex-nun could really understand the adjustment process. There were many times that we'd be low, or depressed, or frustrated that we'd talk things over and although we might not have solved anything we did comfort each other and made it easier to get through the transition.
>
> * * * * * *
>
> I would talk with her (another ex-nun) about things we had in common, like living at home and getting adjusted to the family, about maturing as a person, about trying to get back in the social swing of things, you know. We were coming from the same place, so to speak, and would share these things.

The maintenance of ties with other former nuns was, as we have said, viewed with ambivalence. Although the benefits of such relations were recognized and admitted, respondents, especially as time went by, became increasingly aware of the costs involved in having former nuns as their only or primary friends. Let us listen to their formulation of the dilemma:

> I have this thing about sticking with former nuns. There's this security thing—I think it's a security measure and I think you don't leave yourself open for other

things to happen. You close that door completely if you are constantly with ex-
nuns who are constantly with other ex-nuns.

* * * * * *

There's a danger in keeping with other ex-nuns. It becomes a crutch and I saw
that I had to change my friendship circle if I was really going to fit back into the
world again.

* * * * * *

I know people who have left and they still manage to meet in groups with other
ex-nuns. They still need to relate to people who lived the same life-style. I don't
see it as a positive thing at all. I see this as the ruination of some of them. They
should get away from it all and not keep going back to the same old thing. It
keeps them from going through the transition. I said to myself that I really didn't
want to get into the bag of running back. You get back into the same thing again,
and you know that it has happened to others.

In evaluating the impact of their circle of friends from religious life,
respondents became increasingly sensitive to the psychological and social
costs of exclusive ties to former nuns. To reduce these costs many began to
make deliberate efforts to include more lay friends and new acquaintances
into their social circle. A few respondents even went so far as to consciously
avoid all contacts with former nuns whenever possible! These actions can be
viewed as conscious efforts by the person-in-transit to exert control over the
direction of her passage and remind us, again, that even in the absence of
institutionalized guidelines social actors prove resilient.

   In addition to these deliberate attempts to make new friends the
composition of the woman's social network also changed as a by-product of
her successful passage to other roles. At work, in the neighborhood, through
dating and marriage, or by joining clubs respondents formed ties to others
based not on past but present roles and situations. If former nuns were of help
in going through some parts of the transition, lay friends were important in
integrating the respondent into existent social structures. They were models
for role playing and sources of information and reward. These new friends,
part of the respondent's ongoing present life, helped to turn the woman's
attention away from her past in the convent and become oriented to the
present and future. If we recall Goode's (1956) definition of adjustment, this
shift in friends becomes significant as one index of successful transition to
secular life. As a perceptive respondent observes:

   I think someone's adjusted well to the transition if she has new friends—people
   who were not in the convent also. If you're still hanging around just with other
   ex-nuns, then I wouldn't say that you've made it really.

   Although making new friends certainly suggests some measure of
integration into their present secular environment, it is not necessary that
respondents relinquish completely their ties to other former nuns in order for
us to speak of accommodation to new roles and life-styles. Conceptually, we
can seek to determine if the *bases* of the respondents' relations to their friends
from religious life remain rooted in shared past experiences and roles or

become grounded in present ones. This distinction is also suggested by Goode's (1956) examination of the postdivorce social adjustment of his respondents: "We do not expect them to forget the past: We are simply asking whether they are solving the problems of their new postion or status, rather than reliving the old" (p.241). In looking over the interview data with Goode's question in mind, I examined the content of the conversation shared between respondents and their ex-nun friends. I had asked respondents to describe what topics of conversation most frequently emerged when they got together with other former nuns.

Their answers were coded into two categories suggested by Glaser and Strauss (1971) in the following observation on passages:

> Desirable status passages are subject to recapitulations by passagee and agents for several reasons—which in turn are based on two general purposes: a combination of a sentimental journey back to re-enjoy aspects of the passage and to control either the forward shape of the same or a new passage.   (p.97)

According to Glaser and Straus, when persons-in-passage gather with others who may be going through the same passage or who are helping them through a passage, two types of "recapitulations" may be present in their conversations. The "sentimental recapitulation" serves "to re-enjoy aspects of the passage." For our study this meant conversations that recalled the good times shared in the convent and reminiscing about the enjoyable experiences and memorable events of bygone days. Two quotations illustrate this sentimental recapitulation:

> When a group of us are together, who haven't been together for awhile, we talk about it (the convent days) and laugh about the things that went on.
> * * * * * *
> It was fun to go back over the crazy things we did, how we got into trouble, the good things we did—we'd have a good laugh.

The second type, termed "instrumental recapitulation," served "to discover where the desirable passage went wrong or broke down. *Critical review* is made of a once desirable passage to fix fault, negligence, or blame" (Glaser & Strauss, 1971). A respondent who found this type of recapitulation too frequent and too undesirable among her friends says: "it was almost as though they couldn't get it (the convent days) out of their minds. They were very bitter and they would all get into these things of 'she did this' and 'somebody didn't do that'."

Using Glaser and Strauss' typology of recapitulations two relationships emerged in analyzing the data. First, motives for leaving were related to the type of recapitulation engaged in by respondents. Women who left religious life for ideological reasons—who were "pushed out" into an environment that they really did not prefer—were more likely to engage in the "critical review" served by the instrumental recapitulation. They were angry, bitter, disappointed, and frustrated and made this known to their friends by frequent negative references to persons and events in religious life. Sentimental recapitulations were engaged in more frequently by those who wanted to leave for personal reasons and who were attracted to secular life. They carried with them more favorable memories of their past religious life and looked forward to reliving them in pleasant conversation.

Secondly, I found that for most respondents the frequency with which the past convent days were the topic of conversation when former nuns got together decreased the longer they were out and the more expanded their set of roles and activities had become. Both the desire and the need to refer to the past decreased as they became involved in new relations and new experiences. This is true for both types of recapitulations and suggests that the base of one's ties to friends who were also former nuns changes, over time, to a contemporary foundation. Listen to one respondent depict this change:

> At first V., L., and I used to talk about the convent a lot. We'd exchange gossip and rumors and like it was as if that's all we had in common. It's really different now. We hardly ever mention the convent, except if something big has happened, but none of us really cares about it anymore. It's the past. Now we talk about our jobs and men and vacations, and we relate to each other as friends, not as ex-nuns.

In terms of assessing the impact of friendship networks on transitional adjustment we have seen that different types of friendship circles were salient at specific stages in the transition and served distinct functions for the respondents. It was also noted that the kinds of bases on which prior friendships are sustained is an important consideration in understanding accommodations to social roles. If we are conceptualizing adjustment as a process by which one comes to see oneself and act in terms of present and future roles, then the making of new friendships and altering the bases of old ones not only aids in this process but is a clue to its ongoing presence.

A final theme, repeated with variations throughout this chapter, should also be stressed. The ways in which respondents negotiated the transition to intimacy underscores a point often ignored in the social sciences; namely, that the behaviors and meanings of social actors are shaped by *present* demands and *future* orientations as well as by *prior* experience and early training. Our linear, deterministic modes of thinking often make us place considerable importance on a person's past background of experience and learning to the neglect of how present expectations and future projections come to play a part in shaping social behavior. One result of this shift in emphasis would be a move away from the more deterministic theories of human behavior toward those which capture the dynamic, voluntaristic character of personal and social life.

7
Age, Sex, and Work Roles

As social roles, our age, our sex and the kind of work we do are three significant sources of personal and social identity. Robert A. Nisbet (1970) puts it well: "We tend to identify ourselves to others and to ourselves alike by reference to our social roles and the greater or lesser success we feel that we have in these roles."(p.155). These roles are major components of the social structure of a society (Banton, 1965, pp.33–34) and are social locations around which many of our experiences and relationships are grounded and find their meaning. These three roles differ among themselves in many ways, perhaps the most frequently observed one being the ascribed nature of age and sex roles and the achieved nature of the work role.[1] Beyond their differences, however, all three are of major significance in our society in shaping identity and social behavior as basic social roles, and for this reason are considered together in this chapter.

In earlier chapters we have already introduced some of the implications of the respondents' age, sex, and work roles for relinquishing religious life and making the transition to emotional and sexual intimacy. Here we wish to explore more fully the respondents' transition to their age, sex, and work roles. Rather than assume them as given, we are taking as problematic—as something to be explained—the former nuns' transition to their roles as adults, women, and workers.

While there are important connections between these three transitions, for the purpose of analytical clarity we will discuss each one separately.

---

[1]While age and sex roles are universally ascribed, the work role is achieved in certain societies and ascribed in others (Nisbet, 1970, pp. 156–157).

AGE ROLES

Let us begin with age and recall that, by virtue of having been in religious life anywhere from five to more than fifteen years, these women did not move with their age peers through the typical sequences of experience and roles usually associated with age categories. They lagged behind their age peers in many spheres of life—as lovers, mothers, workers, students. Their age passage has been arrested (Glaser & Strauss, 1971, p.31) and will pose for them special problems of accountability and accommodation, because age is more than just a chronological reality. It is, as Riley et al. (1972, pp.413–414) observe, "a generalized status" or role which contains expectations of persons, in different age categories, to be certain kinds of people. The terms we use for age categories—child, teenager, young adult, mature adult— convey these expectations of how we should present ourselves to others and the kinds of behavior we can expect from them. A person's age, then, appears to have attached to it an array of expectations predictive of behavior, sentiment, knowledge, and ability. The phrase, "acting one's age," comes close to a commonsense understanding of age as a social role which influences exchanges between persons.

Specifically, adult women and men in our society are expected to be capable of managing their personal appearance, familiar with socializing, able to handle financial and household matters, comfortable in sexual and romantic situations, as well as having a range of other experiences and understandings that conventional adulthood implies. Earlier we mentioned that respondents were aware of how religious life arrested aspects of this passage to adulthood. Every one of them expressed some variation on the theme of arrested age passage. According to them, life in the convent, to varying degrees, fostered a childlike dependency on others, an inability to feel confident in one's opinions and choices, an adolescent self-consciousness, and an overall immaturity unsuited to adulthood. A respondent who had been out for less than one year observes:

> In many ways I'm eighteen years old really, because I've been in religious life for sixteen years and there are some things I do that are like a teenager. Sixteen years is a long time, even if things have changed in the past five to ten years. There's still a long time to account for, to make up for, and I know that I have to grow up in some ways.

In addition to this perceived psychological immaturity respondents expressed ignorance of the social expectations for their appropriate age roles. Given their age, how should they act, feel, look, think? Three women, ranging in age from twenty-six to thirty-seven, comment on their initial ignorance of age-related expectations and their ability to "act one's age":

In other ways I kid and say that I really have teenybopper taste; like I sometimes worry about not wearing clothes that are suitable for someone my age. Like I don't want to make a fool out of myself.

* * * * * *

Here I was in a situation that young adults should even be good at—opening up a checking account! I was thirty-two and should have had this experience and yet I felt so foolish doing this, asking questions that a teenager would be asking.

* * * * * *

I don't feel that I have the poise, the self-confidence, that knowledge that a thirty-seven year old woman would have. I still feel and act like I'm twenty-one and I suppose it'll take time for me to "season".

As these quotations illustrate, the former nun enters the transitional period aware that age expectations exist, although not always certain as to their specific content. Within just a few weeks of being back in the lay world she soon discovers that *others* will begin to invoke such expectations in their relationship with her. For example, one thirty-year-old respondent reports on tension between her and her dating partner arising because "he still feels like I'm acting as a teenager and he told me so a few times. I try to catch myself, but sometimes I'm not sure I even see it, although now I'm getting better at it." Another former nun, at the age of twenty-four, reports that her friend "told me my clothes were too old-looking for my age—that I didn't dress to fit my age." A member of one family chides a thirty-four-year-old respondent for "always being so moody and indecisive, just like a teenager in an identity crisis." In terms of both personal identity and social exchange the former nun was challenged to learn about, and become expert in producing, the behaviors expected of her age role. At the same time, however, she did not wish to appear naive, nor did she always want to "account" for her naivete by revealing the fact that she was a former nun.

How did these women accumulate the knowledge of age expectations and solicit evaluations of their performances in these roles? The major impersonal source of useful information was found in newspapers, television, magazines, and other mass media channels. A respondent recalls "reading *Cosmopolitan* and *McCalls* to get a range of ideas about what women my age were thinking about, talking about, wearing." The women "did their homework," as one put it, by reading, window-shopping, and listening for clues to age expectations.

Personal relationships were the other major source of both information and evaluation. Different tactics were taken by the respondent depending on whether or not others knew she was once a nun. With persons who were aware of the respondent's religious past, she could be candid about inquiries regarding age-related expectations: "I would ask my friend F. if she thought I looked alright, or I would describe something that happened at work to my sister and ask her if I handled it in a mature, realistic way." Family members, especially female siblings, were a major channel of knowledge and a trusted set of critics. Others, such as lay friends and former nuns who had been out of religious life for longer periods of time, made similar contributions.

In front of strangers, however, or those to whom the respondent did not want her past revealed, she was more discreet in picking up age-related expectations:

> (When you say that you looked at others for clues what do you mean?)
> Well, like at my job I would watch how the girls at work would react with one another, how they acted toward their work and just socializing, and I would compare, I guess, my behavior with them. In that sense I would say they were giving me clues for my own behavior.
> * * * * * *
> When I was in the convent we used to see some catalogues and find out what the fashions were, but when I went out to buy clothes after I left I bought collegiate clothes, like the ones I wore when I was in college rather than what the style was at this time. Like those years in the convent were just lost. (How did you realize this?) When I started working, I looked at the other women and saw that they were dressed differently than I was.
> * * * * * *
> I would listen intently to conversations between people and try to see how they reacted to situations, what things meant to them at their age.

This unobtrusive reading of "proper" behavior gave the former nun a wider circle of people who could serve as her inadvertent agents of socialization and models for age roles.

In addition to age as a generalized social position, we know that there also exist particular age criteria for occupying other roles or engaging in particular types of behavior. For example, we expect that going to college, being married for the first time, beginning to work, and other activities will be done by people at certain ages. Our respondents did not conform to many of these taken-for-granted expectations. Many were chronologically adult women who were having their first dates, sexual encounters, and marriages. Others, especially those who were single women and thus not "excused" from assuming certain roles and experiences, were even more of an anomaly; they were going on their first job interviews, earning their first salaries, establishing their first credit references, acquiring their first apartments.

Riley et al. (1972, p.413) have provided us with an important concept, "age incongruity," to refer to these violations "of age-related expectations or of age criteria for role incumbency." That age incongruity leads to both psychological strain as well as interactional difficulty is suggested by the interview data. Respondents, in describing their earliest reactions to secular role playing, admit to having felt self-conscious, awkward, and hesitant in such "new" situations. They had no reservoir of accumulated experiences and tested expectations that make for confidence in age-role performance:

> Well, this was the first time I had ever went to look for a job and went on interviews and I was scared. They asked me what organizations I belonged to

and what my interests were and if I had ever traveled and I just didn't know how to answer them. They asked me what salary I wanted and I didn't even know anything about salaries and I felt so foolish.

* * * * * *

I was very tense going into department stores. I felt so conspicuous like I really didn't belong there and everybody was looking at me and knew it. Maybe I was a bit paranoid. (Why did you feel that way?) Well, the salesgirl would ask what size I wore and I didn't know and she'd give me a look. I mean here were all these other people who knew all these things and were so self-assured.

* * * * * *

I can remember one of the first times I went to a cocktail party. God, was I a nervous wreck! This may sound silly, but I didn't know how to engage in cocktail talk, in smalltalk. Now I do, but then it was awful. I felt so ill at ease with those people, not knowing what to say that was clever and witty and not deep.

* * * * * *

I was thirty-one going on my second date and I felt like thirteen. I was asking myself, "Should I sit close to him?" "What will I do if he wants to kiss me?" I mean it was a real trauma for me, and it's only now that I can laugh at it all.

In exchanges with others there was also evidence of interactional strain as age-incongrous behavior threw *others* off balance, caused them embarrassment, and generated confusion. A former nun reports that fellow teachers at work perceived her lack of participation in discussions about men and romance, and her unwillingness to join them for end-of-the-week gatherings at a local bar as signs of her aloofness and prudery. Another respondent entering her first marriage at the age of thirty-eight recalls the awkwardness of her friends who had assumed she was a divorced woman. In discussing an early dating partner a respondent remembers her partner's sense of unease, "like he knew I was somehow different, inexperienced, but he couldn't pinpoint why. I didn't make sense to him." These comments underscore the relational nature of social roles and some of the interactional problems that arise when persons violate role expectations.

Our final consideration of the matter of age incongruity concerns its implications for "passing" (Goffman, 1963,p.73). As Goffman (1963) points out, "Because of the great rewards in being considered normal, almost all persons who are in a position to pass will do so on some occasion by intent" (p.74). To anticipate our discussion of the stigmatizing attributes of the role of ex-nuns, let us say here that, for various reasons, almost every respondent preferred to "pass" as a normal woman at some time, or under certain conditions, or with particular persons. However, age incongruity threatened successful passing to the extent that the respondent was suspected of being something different than she presented herself to be and an "account" (Scott & Lyman, 1963) of her behavior was necessary. Examples of this dilemma abound in the interviews—a dating partner is curious as to why a respondent, seemingly attractive and "healthy," has had so little dating experience; a banker questions the respondent's lack of any of the trappings of consumerism; an acquaintance is curious as to why the respondent has not accumulated any personal belongings after living away from home for so long. When confronted with age incongruity, others may call into question the "virtual social identity" (Goffman, 1963, p. 2) of the individual and jeopardize the chances of successful passing. Younger respondents, in their late twenties, were in a more advantageous position in this regard because they had fewer years to account for and because the discrepancy between age and associated attributes of behavior was not that large. Also, as one younger respondent put it, "It was easier for me at twenty-six to blend into the environment because today there are lots of young adults who are not conforming to the patterns of work and marriage that older adults did." This suggests that changes in the larger system may also affect the variable degree to which age-incongruity may generate problems for the individual-in-a-role and the further possibility that age-related expectations themselves are undergoing revision.[2]

When respondents are grouped according to length of the time they have been out of the convent we note that the longer the respondent has been out, the more confident she feels in playing her age role and the fewer of her reports of age incongruity. This holds true regardless of her chronological age and the length of time spent in religious life. We interpret this to imply that exposure to role expectations, motivations to learn appropriate behavior, and actual participation in social roles may be as, or more, important in successful transition than the impact of past socialization or such "givens" as chronological age.

Commonsense wisdom regarding the inflexibility of the older person in our society has increasingly been contested by both older citizens themselves as well as by current research on aging (Clausen, 1972; Riley, et al., 1972; Rosow, 1975). The findings from this study also indicate that chronological age, in and of itself, is not a major determinant of the person's response to her present situation or her aspirations for the future. Our data point to a number of variables in the transitional phase that are more important than age in shaping the former nun's accommodation to secular roles. We have stated that the length of time the respondent has been out of the convent is associated with the successful transition to secular roles. This is a gross variable that subsumes more specific ones, such as the amount of time one has to discover role expectations, to practice role performances and receive evaluations from others of one's presentation of self, to build a repertoire of social skills and experiences, and to begin to define oneself in terms of these new roles. It is these more specific and dynamic variables that account for much of the variation in respondents' ability to pick up arrested passages in the transitional phase. This is not to imply, of course, that age is irrelevant as an explanatory factor. We have, in fact, indicated that the respondent's age

---

[2]See, for example, Atwater (1973).

influenced her decision to relinquish religious life, her perceived abilities to make the transition and her access to people and events that facilitated the transition. Nevertheless, an overemphasis on age as merely a structural chronological variable does an injustice to the subjective meanings age has for respondents; in addition, it obscures the part played by other factors in explaining respondents' accommodations to social roles.

SEX ROLES

A person's gender as female or male is assigned by others at birth and generally is understood to be an ascribed characteristic. While gender refers to physical attributes, sex roles refer to the cluster of social expectations deemed appropriate for how women and men should behave (Chafetz, 1974, pp.1–5). The roles of women and men and the definitions of their behavior as feminine and masculine are social constructions rather than biological givens. These roles and definitions are established by society and learned by individuals, beginning at infancy.

It is a basic sociological truth that all roles, including sex roles, are never static; they continue to be revised to meet changing societal and individual needs (Banton, 1965, pp.42–67). The role of woman (and indirectly that of man) has, since the mid-sixties, been undergoing exactly such change. There is no longer any doubt that there is presently moving through our society a vigorous, determined, and ideologically informed assault on traditional sex roles. This social movement, known as feminism, has raised important questions about the impact of traditional sex roles on identity and personality development (Bardwick, 1971; Maccoby & Jacklin, 1974); on the quality of relationships between and among the sexes (Brownmiller, 1975; Farrell, 1974; Freeman, 1975), and on the distribution along sex lines of privilege and power in the larger society (Kelly & Boutilier, 1978; Safilios-Rothschild, 1974; Whitehurst, 1977). This changing role of woman elicits the following question in the context of our study of former nuns: What happens to people when the role that they are trying to learn and to play with conviction is itself undergoing profound alteration in the society at large?

All of us reading this book are, to varying degrees, grappling with the same question. But women who once were nuns are in a unique position. As we indicated in Chapter 4, during much of their lives as nuns, these women subordinated their sex role to the more generalized and pervasive demands of the religious role. Being a nun meant being a celibate woman for whom the ordinary experiences and roles of lay women were either forbidden or unimportant.[3] Paradoxically, while a nun was discouraged, through convent

---

[3]In a perspective observation, Ebaugh (1977, p. 24) interprets the fact that the novice frequently received a male name, such as Sister Mark or Sister Mary Robert, as a formal indication that "sexual differences were no longer emphasized."

laws, ideology, vows, and routines, from defining herself and acting in terms of her role as a woman, the very same structure of convent life, grounded in Catholic theology, reinforced traditional feminine values and behavior.

Over the past few years a considerable amount of literature has appeared which criticizes religion and religious organizations as sexist in consequence, if not intent (Bullough,1973; Doely, 1970; Hageman, 1974). Theologians such as Rosemary Ruether (1974) and Mary Daly (1975) have become well known for their feminist analyses of such questions as the ordination of women, the patriarchal underpinnings of religious traditions, the cult of Mary, and the subordinate position of women in the church. While more has been written about the Christian religions, the position of women in Judaism is also undergoing scrutiny (Koltun, 1976) as a religion grounded in patriarchal beliefs, laws, and traditions.

I believe this feminist framework is essential to understanding the paradoxical nature of the nun as woman and its consequences for the former nun's resumption of her role as a secular woman. The culture and social organization of the Roman Catholic Church, and religious orders in particular, are permeated with sexism. The imagery, symbols, language, roles, and structure of authority defined as sexist are evident, for example, in comparing the roles of priest and nun.[4] "Father" is superior to "Sister" in authority; his major functions are "sacred" and grounded in the Sacraments, while hers are not; he can own property and have private monies, she cannot; he can drink and smoke and go out alone, she cannot; he can exercise independence, freedom of choice,and individuality while she must always be a part of the larger "community" and subordinate herself to her order.

The process by which a woman was socialized to become a nun provides us with a clear and unequivocal instance of conditioning women to traditional "female" attributes, virtues, skills, and orientations. She is taught to be passive, subordinate, submissive, collectivity-oriented, nurturant, quiet, childlike, pure, hard-working, and obedient. She is publicly a paragon of virtue—"the good Sister" who teaches the children and cares for the poor and sick; she is to be unassuming, restrained, innocent; she is to be beyond the worldly vices of anger, competition, pettiness, self-interest, laziness, sexuality, and materialism that flaw the secular individual. She embodies, or is taught and thought to embody, the essential female complex of values, attitudes, and behavior.

Thus, the nun, although living outside the mainstream of secular female culture, was nonetheless socialized to a religious role and participated in an organization that closely approximated the society's patriarchal themes. This is a crucial observation because it sheds light on the issue before us; namely, as nuns left the convent and assumed their roles as secular women they had a

---

[4]Although recent changes in religious life have lessened some of these differences between priest and nun the general comparison remains valid even today.

choice as to which kind of woman they could be. They could resume the society's more traditional female role or could opt for the emerging role of women that was being created through the feminist movement.

In doing my research for this book during the early seventies, the peak years of this emergent feminist consciousness, I had hypothesized that former nuns would be more likely to embrace the newer vision of women than the more traditional one. Why? My prediction was based on a certain way of looking at religious life. A religious order can be viewed as one of the rare social organizations where women freely choose to organize, staff, coordinate, and play out their lives without men and motherhood—those two major coordinates that socially locate the woman in every society. Here is a genuine, radical feminist experiment: women working, eating, sleeping, creating, producing, deciding, defining, playing, praying—in sum, living by themselves with other women. If this is one's conception, and to some extent it contains much empirical validity, then one might expect former nuns to enter the secular world ready to assume the newer configuration of the role of woman. I expected them to respond favorably to this role that stresed independence, self-assertion, achievement, and nonfamilistic life-style choices. The findings failed to support my hypothesized prediction. As will soon be evident, the respondents' resumption of their sex role was carried out according to the more traditional vision of the woman's role. Upon examining the above model of religious life I came to see several errors in this conceptualization which help explain its failure to correctly predict the respondents' behavior.

First, as I mentioned earlier, the culture and social organization of convent life was shaped along the same sexist lines as those of secular institutions of the larger society. These structures, and the process of socializing women to them, were of great importance in sustaining traditional feminine behavior and values. Second, the ability to define oneself in feminist terms and to interpret one's situation within a feminist framework requires at least that one be aware of oneself as a woman. Regarding respondents' self-conception, we have seen that their awareness of themselves as women was by and large suppressed under the "master status" (Hughes, 1945) of being a nun. Third, I had erroneously assumed that nuns *chose* a single, celibate, single-sexed community life-style. The fact of the matter is, however, that respondents *chose to become nuns* and this life-style was the required condition for being able to be officially accepted as a nun. Finally, and perhaps most importantly for understanding their subsequent adherence to a more traditional model of woman, I had not considered the possibility that these respondents were looking forward to the "benefits" of being women so long denied them while in religious life. Insofar as their goal was to become women again—in the sense in which sex role is a basic axis of self-identity and social membership—assuming the stance of a "liberated woman" could jeopardize this goal. Put bluntly, one's acceptance as a woman by others is not gotten by being autonomous, competitive, rational, achieving, assertive, and the like. In most parts of society, even today, the "women's libber," as she is referred to, has her credibility as a woman cast into doubt.[5] For former nuns, who desired acceptance as women and whose ability to make transitions to other roles was dependent on this acceptance, their choice of the traditional female role was clearly understandable.

We are now prepared to explore the process by which former nuns resumed active roles as women in secular society. One of the first strategies they employed was what we can call "body work"—a set of activities designed to bring the body, appearance, and overall physical impression in line with the female role. They experimented with different hairstyles, bought clothes, practiced putting on makeup, had their ears pierced, went on diets, and in various ways sought to present public images of themselves as everyday women. As Scott and Lyman (1963, p. 33) observe, "since individuals are aware that appearances may serve to credit or discredit accounts, efforts are understandably made to control their appearances through a vast repertoire of impression management activities." One area where respondents had total control over their situation was precisely in the area of physical impression and much effort went into it. But even such a simple matter as this is problematic at first, as these comments reveal:

> I started to lose weight, learned how to put on makeup, which was really funny, practicing in front of a mirror; I'd dab it on and look like a clown. I also learned to set my hair and sometimes I looked pretty awful. I worked on my clothes—a friend helped me buy shoes, clothes, jewelry. I really don't know if I could have done without that kind of help in the beginning. I really didn't know much at first.

* * * * * *

> It was really funny now when I look at it, but not then, when we had to go into the stores and of course we didn't have much money to spend and we'd go into the stores where everybody dressed in front of everybody else. (How did you feel about that?) That was a traumatic experience. I remember going into the dressing room with three or four pairs of slacks because I really didn't know what size I wore. It was pretty bad.

* * * * * *

> There were so many things I had to learn, like which styles fit me for my build and my age and which colors were flattering. My sister would go shopping with me in the beginning to help pick things out.

Ironically, while many secular women were taking off their makeup, letting their hair return to natural colors and easy-to-keep-styles, gaining control of their bodies through sport and other "nonfeminine" activities these women

---

[5]This fact may help to explain such intriguing phenomena as the frequent denial by achieving women (in politics, business, the military, etc.) that they are feminist or are concerned with larger feminist issues, or the exaggerated use of "feminine" accouterments (make-up, ribbons, jewelry, style of uniforms) by successful women athletes.

were reverting to physical activities that were targeted as "objectifications of the female" (Millum, 1975) by the feminist movement.[6] Through trial and error, observation of others, and assistance from friends and family, respondents began to shape their appearance in accord with their traditional image of themselves as women. An interesting observation made by two women suggests that some measure of their movement through transitional stages is reflected in changes in personal attire and attitudes toward one's body:

> I wasn't really in tune with my body and I think it took a while. It was a very gradual thing. Like that first summer out I got a one-piece bathing suit, last summer I had a regular two-piece bathing suit, and this summer I have a bikini and in my own mind I see that and feel that this is my transition and I often laugh.
>
> * * * * * *
>
> When I compare the type of clothes I bought when I first left and those I buy now there's such a difference that I think it must say something about where I've come from. (Could you explain this?) Well my earlier clothes were too big for me, they were drab and in dark colors—very subdued, conservative. My style has changed; I now know what I like and I'm willing to experiment.

As a result of participating in a secular environment where being a woman is a salient feature of everyday life, respondents began to increasingly refer to other women for standards of evaluation. Their involvement in roles and activities which contain norms for sex-role participation made them increasingly attentive to sources for assessing their own performances as women. A respondent captures this more concentrated attention by remarking, "I'm now more likely to look at other women—how they're dressed, how they carry themselves, what they say—and compare myself to them. There was little need to do that in the convent." As time goes by, women, precisely as women, become more significant as reference points for the respondent, which helps to underscore her attachment to the female role and bring her behavior and sentiment in closer alignment with the role. A former nun who had been out for about two years compares herself now as a woman with when she was a nun and observes, "I'm not ashamed to express my emotions now. I am learning to respond more like a woman." Another suggests that, "I have become more interested in womanly things—cooking, shopping, clothes, sex—and to read and discuss these things with other women." Still another comments that "even my thinking has changed in the sense that as a nun I used to be more logical, more rational; I believe I thought like a man and now I feel I am looking at things in more than just rational terms."

Even in the management of their other role transitions respondents worked to integrate them into support of their role as women. Although we shall

---

[6]I am indebted to Dr. Mary Boutilier for this observation.

discuss the articulation of multiple roles in Chapter 9, we might briefly note its occurrence here. Specifically, success in one role may bring confidence in playing others. Just as all roles receive social confirmation and are activated when they elicit appropriate responses from others, a major validation of being a woman is to have men react in anticipated ways (Safilios-Rothschild, 1977). To be whistled at, to be told one is pretty, to be asked for a date are unequivocal signals that others see you as a woman and function to increase one's confidence in that role. Part of the motivation to date and part of the anxiety over not dating that comes across in many interviews is tied to this issue of wanting to validate one's claim to being a woman. This is succinctly stated by a former nun who expressed much concern with the initial absence of dating activity during the first year she was out: "I also wanted to date because it helped me know I was attractive to men—that I was a woman." Success in dating and sexual intimacy served to increase the respondent's confidence in herself as a woman and thus facilitate the resumption of her sex role.

Other respondents were also aware that what was happening in other areas of their transition—where they resided, who their friends were, where they worked—had consequences for their successful resumption of the female role:

> I wanted to get a job very badly because I knew that without it I couldn't buy clothes and things that would help me be attractive as a woman and not look like an ex-nun.
>
> * * * * * *
>
> I deliberately began to cultivate women friends who were not ex-nuns because they knew the woman's world and could help me discover it. My friends were ex-nuns; we were all in the same boat and really couldn't help each other out that much.

These activities can be seen as somewhat conscious efforts by respondents to engage in behavior that is supportive of their roles as women. By deliberately manipulating other parts of her passage—work, dating, friendship—she could strengthen her sex-role presentation.

The interview materials we have presented to illustrate ideas about sex role accommodations can be reread to shed light on the respondents' conception of the female role. Most respondents generally accepted a traditional image of women with its emphasis on the primacy of marriage and children; the existence of "natural differences" between the sexes in terms of sentiment, modes of thinking, and biological drives; and the belief that the sexes do, and should continue to, inhabit somewhat distinct spheres of existence regarding work, leisure, community participation, child-rearing, governing, and the like. Only one respondent held to a model of woman that can be called feminist, and she apparently had formulated her conception of being a woman long before entering religious life as a result of early family socialization. With the exception of agreeing to "equal work for equal pay," the majority of respondents were fairly uncritical of the content of institutionalized sex roles.

In examining the interview data I did find a few respondents who had left religious life with traditional images of the female role and had begun to reevaluate these ideas in the light of their immediate experiences in the secular community. These respondents were approximately thirty years old; they were single; they had been out of the convent for two to three years; they had relatively active social lives; and they expressed satisfaction with their jobs. Once these women discovered that they could, in fact, build for themselves an independent and satisfying life-style, the pressure they felt earlier to follow the path of traditional women began to decrease and be replaced by a wish to leave their present plans open-ended. These women, like the other respondents, had been very concerned about what would happen to them after leaving religious life. They keenly felt the absence of any permanent ties or plans that give most people a feeling of security for the years that stretch before them. Many of them echoed this theme by noting that "at least in the convent you knew what the rest of your life was going to be like; you had that security." It is still true today that for many, many women the life-plan that is available in the female role points to marriage, children, and noncareer employment. Once, however, some of these women begin to experience success and rewards in pursuing alternate styles of existence, they are able to question their attachment to the ideas of what women can and should be. This reevaluation is described in dynamic terms by a very observant respondent:

> It's hard to say what factors began to influence my thinking about women's role in society. When I first left I felt I just had to find a man, get married, settle down. Maybe this was a reaction against not having the security of convent life. But really, I didn't think of any options and was pretty desperate for awhile. As I began to do things on my own and to do them—my finances, the job, new friends, and dating men—well, maybe I became more confident in myself, and more willing to think that there are options for women besides the ones we're taught by society. You come to realize that you, as a person and as a woman, can make your own way, even if it's hard at times.

These changing conceptions of woman's role seem to me to be more a result of altered social experiences than of intellectual or ideological conversion to feminism as a belief system. This implies that for ideological shifts to occur in how women respond to roles they must be backed up by personal experience that is valued and effective. Women must continue to be encouraged to play new roles, have new experiences, and join new groups so that they can test for themselves the degree of satisfaction and effectiveness possible in moving beyond the present boundaries of woman's role. Exposure to feminist ideology, either in the form of intellectual analysis or political rhetoric, is not sufficient for producing sustained change in one's personal and social life as a woman.

A final issue we wish to consider in examining sex roles is the changing quality of the respondents' relationship with other women once they return to secular society. It has been frequently noted that as a consequence of sex-role stereotyping and sexist culture women are encouraged to view one another in hostile, suspicious, and competitive ways (Pogrebin, 1972; Sherif, 1974). Certain social scientists (Tiger, 1969) even argue that the absence of "bonding" among women is rooted in our biological makeup. We have all been told that women dislike other women and lack the bond of intensity and centrality that allegedly exists between men. Ongoing research is producing findings that partially dispel the myth of male camaraderie and hostility among women (Aries, 1977; Booth, 1972). Nevertheless, it remains true that at least as early as adolescence, and continuing over the life-cycle, women are encouraged to view other women as competitors for the scarce rewards attached to the female role—physical attractiveness, sexual desirability, male companionship, marriage, and children (Chafetz, 1974, p. 184).

What happens, then, when some women, such as nuns, remove themselves from the social environment in which these rewards are salient and join with one another in an all-female community in which relationships are based on grounds other than those dominated by male reaction and evaluation? Do these women develop different kinds of relations with one another than their secular peers? From the interview data, we already established that the salience of her sex role is diminished in religious life. In probing for the kinds of relations these women had with one another while in the convent we came upon rather interesting and wide-ranging responses. The majority of former nuns indicated there was little or no competition between them and other nuns in terms of being women. Reflecting on her experiences in the convent a former nun recalls:

> When you were in the convent you would hear on the outside, maybe in your own family, of how a woman would be jealous of this woman, and you'd say, "Oh, gosh! How could that be?" That really never bothered you when you were in because there was no reason to compete with other women in that way. But, when you get out, you just see it. It is so evident, and women are so catty and petty. Competing, to me, is so unimportant.

Yet, other respondents clearly recall the existence of competition among some nuns. One respondent observes:

> Oh, I'd say that there were nuns who were very conscious of how they looked and would compete with one another in subtle ways. I remember that a young attractive Sister would wear her cap closer to her eyes because she looked better that way. I would press pleats in the front of my habit because I wanted it to fit closer and look smarter. We were conscious of our looks and dress and watched how others looked.

Another woman, in discussing the impact of going into modified habits, makes an observation that not only affirms the presence of some competition for physical attractiveness, but also strengthens our earlier finding that changes in religious garb served to heighten one's role as a woman:

It was really something when the habits changed. Many nuns were vying with one another for the most interesting colors and styles. Some nuns had whole wardrobes of different collars, in different styles and colors. There were lots of comparisons over who looked better.

Although there is disagreement among respondents over the amount of invidious "feminine" competition there is much more consensus over the fact that jealousy, competition, and striving existed to capture the rewards offered by the religious community itself—power, position, privilege, popularity, and recognition:

We may not have envied others for the things that most women have, but there were struggles and competition over being a Principal, or Superior, for example, or getting a good grade to teach, or being popular with the parishioners—things like that.

* * * * * *

It's hard to say how much we competed as women, but there was competition and envy between us for other things. (What kinds of things?) Like being a Superior, having more say over community life, getting better job assignments.

As these comments suggest, although there might have been less concern over seeking the rewards of one's sex role, there clearly were contests for accruing to oneself the gains available in the social system the nuns were operating in. The significance of this finding, then, is the realization that competition, jealousy, and striving occurred among *nuns* rather than among *women*: that is, the culture and organization of a social system fosters certain kinds of relations among people, these relations being neither biologically determined or psychologically "given."

Virtually all respondents observed that it was difficult to sustain the intense, close relationships with secular women that they once had with women in religious life. One woman who had been in the lay world for four years makes this point:

You can't have relations with women on the outside like you did in the convent. Things are so different and you yourself change. I find myself now in more competition with women, or at least I feel that they view me as a competitor. I'm sort of more aware of them now than I was before, I guess because now I'm in the market, so to speak, for romance.

Secular society activates one's sex role; it encourages change not continuity, diversity rather than uniformity; it is not the convent society and it cannot sustain those types of relationships:

I do notice and do feel that my relations with women are more intense, strong, intimate, and less competitive than the usual relations women have with one another. Something that I find missing or lacking is just this in the secular world. The relations between women are kind of superficial compared to the relationships you formed in the convent. This nitty-natty kind of stuff really gets on my nerves. (Nitty-natty?) Those superficial relationships, based on expediency.

* * * * * *

> When I think of the person I mentioned who is still in—and I was so close to her for four and one-half years—well, I haven't spoken to any one person as much now. I have some close friends here but it's not the same because I guess my life has expanded in a sense. Like I have friends in different locations who mean a lot to me, but not in the all-encompassing way that B. was. In that way, things have changed. Like B. was everything in a sense to me. She was the bulwark. I would call her for anything and in that way things have changed.

Most, but not all, respondents accepted this change in the nature of their relations with secular women as appropriate to their new lives as women and "as inevitable if you really are going to get back into the outside world." They did not differ from the few who resisted this change in terms of such variables as marital status, motive for leaving, age, or extent of active social life. The one variable that did differentiate them is that those few respondents who began to change their traditional image of women's role were the ones who wanted to maintain the more intense relationships they used to have with women. Their gradual acceptance of new ways to be women included a reassessment of accepted relations among women as well as between the sexes.

We end our discussion of the transition to sex roles with two sociological impressions. First, regarding the nature of sex-role identity and relations between the sexes it becomes apparent that the kind of identities and relationships it is possible to generate and sustain in one setting are susceptible to alteration once persons are in different systems of action, playing different roles. This is as true for sex-role identity as it is for the other social identities and roles that we embrace. Second, in terms of women's relations with women, we expect them to continue to undergo qualitative changes as traditional sex-role images decline and as women begin to base their ties to one another not only in male-centered terms, but also through the wide range of activities and roles that extend beyond the relations between the sexes.

WORK ROLES

The last part of this chapter concentrates on the respondents' assumption of work roles in the secular society. Similar to age and sex roles, a person's work is a significant basis for self-identification and the major social role (Gross, 1958, pp. 3–5). This is especially true for men because, until recently, "women's work" has traditionally been defined as belonging to the spheres of family and homemaking (Appley, 1977; Janeway, 1971). These women were, as nuns, among the few who had pursued the traditionally male sphere of work-as-career. They had vocations to religious life that demanded a full-time "calling" to a profession. To this extent, former nuns were already involved in occupational roles and experiences usually associated with men's role in society. Their ability to play secular work roles was therefore not as problematic for them as the other types of changes they had to adjust to after leaving religious life.

As we mentioned earlier, a few nuns had already received offers of employment before leaving religious life and had made some attempts to "sound out" the secular labor market in anticipation of their leaving. Once they actually had left, they immediately stepped up their efforts to find work. With the help of family members, priests, other former nuns, and lay friends the respondents tried to gather information and opinions about the job market, salaries and benefits, resumes, new openings, and interview behavior. The immediate and pressing financial need to have a job forced a few respondents to take jobs before they had much time to gather proper information and make a satisfactory selection among work offers. To some extent, then, occupational selection was initially a matter of practical expedience.

I divided the respondents into two occupational categories—academic and nonacademic—based on the type of employment they had at the time of the interview. Those who were involved in academic employment, such as teaching, counseling, administration, were viewed as having experienced occupational continuity over their transition from religious to secular roles. Half of the respondents held academic positions, seven held nonacademic ones, and three were unemployed (two of the latter were married and one had just terminated her position). Since all respondents had held academic positions during most of their time in religious life I wanted to explore the causes and consequences of occupational continuity or the lack of it during the transitional phase.

Two factors appeared to be associated with type of occupational choice— the respondent's age and her motivation for leaving the convent. Respondents over the age of thirty-five, those who had spent more time in religious life, were more likely to choose an academic position. They felt that they were "too old to start a new career" and that they had accumulated too much occupational experience and security to give it up for a new career. The continuity between the occupation they held in the convent and the one they had in secular life facilitated some of the problems of work adjustment. They could draw upon the skills, routines, values, and meanings of their past occupational life to meet the demands of their present employment. Younger respondents were somewhat less likely to take academic employment and, as we will discuss, were confronted with different problems posed by occupational discontinuity.

Motivation for leaving religious life was also related to occupational choice. Respondents who left for personal reasons held nonacademic positions. Women who were "pulled" out of the convent by the attractiveness of secular opportunities chose nonacademic positions partially as a means of controlling the direction of their passage to secular life. In describing her refusal to take a teaching position one respondent notes:

I knew I just didn't want to teach because that's all I'd ever done. I really didn't want to— maybe because it reminded me of the convent. I wanted to meet different kinds of people, be doing new things, be involved with the real world, which I felt teaching wouldn't provide me with.

Another spoke of not wanting to teach because "There were so many other options out here, which is the reason I decided to leave, after all." These women purposefully selected occupations that were not associated with convent life as a vehicle for moving into different occupational subcultures which emphasized more secular values, skills, and behavior. These positions were primarily in the business community, civil service, and, to a lesser extent, social service (parole officer, for example).

What were the consequences of such occupational discontinuity? Respondents in nonacademic employment were in positions that were more highly rationalized, instrumental, segmentalized, and impersonal than is usually the case when one teaches primary and secondary school children, or counsels students. These women found themselves in work roles that stressed self-interest, competition, impersonality, and limited emotional commitment. They were unaccustomed to this occupational posture and, at first, devalued it. A former nun working in an insurance company complained about the boring, routine quality of the work; another, employed in a welfare agency, expressed dismay at the selfishness and deceit of work colleagues; a respondent who became a parole officer was shocked at the minimal commitment of people to their clients. The pettiness, gossip, materialism, and "politics" that many of us have become accustomed to in occupational life was met with resistance and disappointment. Their attempt to bring to their new work the meanings, values, and attitudes derived from religious life frustrated these women and they reported greater job dissatisfaction than did respondents with academic employment.

A number of observations can be made about the respondents' career after leaving the convent. Interestingly, getting their first job did not turn out to be as difficult as respondents had anticipated; almost all of them had a position within a month or so of leaving the convent. What they did discover, however, is that as soon as work provided them with sufficient financial security it could be reevaluated in terms of its personal satisfaction and its potential to generate opportunities for playing other roles. Once again we should underscore the respondent's need and desire to take charge of her passage and to be sensitive to the very real interdependence between roles, in this case the connection between work, friendship, finding dating partners, and the like.

Respondents took control over their occupational passage by frequent job changes, amounting, on an average, to one job change approximately every year. Subsequent jobs were chosen not primarily for their financial gain but rather in terms of the quality of work; the ratio of male to female colleagues;

and the perceived possibilities of work leading to new faces, experiences, and places. As a parenthetical note, I interviewed the head of a formal transitional agency for exreligious who informed me that employers "knew" about this "occupational instability" on the part of former nuns and, for this reason, were often hesitant to hire them. In attempting to account for this turnover I have already noted that first jobs were for some a matter of sheer financial expedience and were accepted as temporary measures until economic problems could be settled. I have also suggested that subsequent job changes were deliberate efforts by respondents to control the direction and outcome of their overall transition. Respondents also indicated that job changes were relatively minor in comparison to the larger change in life-style that they were making. One former nun, who had four different jobs in a three-and-one-half-year period said, "People think I'm crazy to keep changing jobs—they ask me if I mind the instability and lack of security. Well, I tell them that compared to the big change I made in leaving the convent, changing jobs is a small thing." I also wonder if, unwittingly, the frequent "house" changes they experienced in religious life, seldom being in the same convent for more than a year or so, made them more accustomed to secular job shifts, insulated them from the disorganizing effects of such changes, and made it easier for them to exert this type of control over the transition. By changing jobs, respondents were able to search for more gratifying work, enlarge their round of experience, accumulate a work record, and, in general, become more integrated into secular life-styles.

It is well known that work, in addition to providing economic stability, serves as a major source of friendship and social group membership. The social compositon of the work setting, then, was significant for helping respondents establish a social life grounded in the ongoing present. Here two related variables—age and stage in the life cycle—have consequences for transitional adjustment. Specifically, the former nun in her late twenties and early thirties who was single found that her occupational career was not in line with those of her age cohort who, at least in the middle class, were more likely to be at home having and rearing children (Harbeson, 1971, pp. 43-44). Her female work colleagues—young girls or newly married young women, older women whose children were now teenagers—were in social locations and at stages in the life course that had little in common with hers. One woman comments on the consequences of this discrepancy for establishing a network of friends:

> Until I got this new job, it was difficult to find people at work who shared my interests and whom I could have as friends. The people I worked with were either girls out of high school talking about their boyfriends, clothes, and family problems or women in their forties and fifties who had teenage children and were in a whole different life-style. I really felt out of place and had nothing in common with them.

Although this employment picture is changing as women, out of desire and need, remain in the labor force during childbearing years (Appley, 1977), this pattern of female employment existing in the early seventies hindered the former nun's chances to draw upon the extraocupational benefits of the work role.

Finally, the data indicate that the longer the respondent had been out of religious life the more likely she was to express satisfaction with her present employment, to name her work colleagues as friends, and to express confidence in her occupational role. It is also significant to note that those values, attitudes, and orientations, once a part of her occupational culture in religious life, became less significant over time. With some ambivalence, three women note the changes in their approach to work, a change away from the collectivity orientation, conscientiousness, and moral commitment that characterized their work as nuns:

> I'm working now with blind children and this is interesting. When I first left, as I told you, I was looking for a focus to my life. There was was no "cause" or anything that guided me and I was dissatisfied. I then would have welcomed anything I could have gotten my teeth into. Now, with this job, there's so much you really could get into, but I'm not that interested anymore.
> * * * * * *
> I'm sure nuns are very conscientious on the jobs when they leave. You were used to doing the job and doing the job well. You went to school whether you felt well or not and you expected other people to be that way too. Now, after being out two years I notice my attitude is changing. I'n not as conscientious as I was. I will take off a day when I need to, even if I'm not sick.
> * * * * * *
> When I first started work I always had to be busy. I felt guilty if I wasn't doing something and would take extra work when mine was finished. That stopped after a while and I found myself acting like the others I work with. I'm not sure I like that though.

These shifts in work orientation were made, to varying degrees, by all respondents. They can serve as further measures of the success respondents are having in making the transition because they reflect a redefinition of work more congruent with the women's present secular life than her past life as a nun.

The following chapter consists of a more theoretical discussion of the issues that have been described and illustrated up to now. We have sketched some of the lines that flesh out the picture of the transitional phase as respondents enter the secular world as adult women, lovers, and workers; a theoretical overview will help as a framework within which to hold these myriad images.

8
Theoretical Overview

The last two chapters portrayed the manner in which respondents experienced and reacted to their immediate postconvent milieu. We explored major substantive areas in the transitional phase and delineated the range of events, both existential and sociological, that mark this phase of the overall passage. In this chapter I wish to develop more explicitly some of the theoretical issues that arise during this phase.

THE TEMPORAL DIMENSION

To speak of a transitional role phase implies, in commonsense usage, a sense of being temporarily suspended between roles. Most people, including sociologists, have difficulty in sustaining a view of social life as constantly changing over increments of time. Specifically with respect to role occupancy, we perceive it as having somewhat fixed temporal benchmarks, as if people can be clearly located as "in" or "out of" a particular role. Our language often obscures the temporal, ever changing nature of role occupancy just as surely as it does the continuous changing of the seasons. Just as we speak of autumn and winter as delineated seasons, we speak of married and divorced as delineated roles. Some sociologists treat role occupancy in much the same manner although others such as Glaser and Strauss (1971) have stressed the theoretical importance of thinking of roles in continuous movement over time. This theme has been stressed in our analysis of the process of role relinquishment and the traditional phases of role acquisitions.

To return for a moment to our analogy of the seasons, at some point we "know" that the transition from autumn to winter has been made. At some point people also "know" that a transition from one role to another has been made. As sociologists, I have suggested that we use the guidelines offered by Goode's conceptualization of adjustment to recognize role occupancy. An obvious question to ask now about this transitional phase is: How long did it last or when did it end? My analysis of the interview data yields an answer similar to the respondents' reply to this very same question which I posed to them. The transitional phase appears to have lasted approximately one year.

This is not to say that full integration into secular life had been accomplished in one year, but rather that by the end of their first year in the larger society every respondent had begun to assume some of the identities and role activities that were part of her present secular life. To varying degrees, each woman had acquired some knowledge of secular role expectations, she took opportunities to practice and to evaluate her performances in these roles, she established new relationships and group affiliations, and she began to define herself as someone other than just a nun or former nun.

The respondents made frequent reference to their first year out of the convent as "the year of transition," "the year of adjustment," and "the transitional period." They estimated that "it took about a year" to become acclaimated to their new life-style as secular women, to have acquired some confidence in living in the secular environment.[1] Even the two women who were interviewed during their first year out estimated that "it'll probably take a good year to really adjust to my new life."

To say that this phase occurs over a year's time may give the erroneous impression that each respondent moved at the same pace in acquiring new identities and social roles. In actuality, although the respondents referred to their first year out as "the year of adjustment," each one established her own tempo and her own private estimate of just how far she had come over the year. Some said it was only a few months before they stopped thinking of themselves as nuns, others said it took longer; some women felt that they had "done better" than they expected in making their initial adjustments while others said it took longer than they had anticipated to become comfortable with their new life-style.

Keeping this in mind, we can say that it is during this first year that much of the learning, experimentation, and evaluation occurs in such a manner and to such a degree that the respondent begins to feel a part of, and a participant in, the secular community. The subsequent years will be devoted to continuing efforts to solidify one's social locations, to improve on role performance, to

---

[1]"One year" is, interestingly, a frequently used temporal benchmark in many societies, including the U.S. Our language includes many references to the twelve month period that includes the cycle of four seasons when we speak of transitions between roles. For example, one year is the customary period for the transitional phases of engagement, mourning, athletic "comeback," medical internships, retirement and the like. Perhaps it is because we expect transitions to take a year that in fact, they often do.

accrue valued rewards for successful role playing, to join new groups, and to affirm new social identities.

THE SELF AS SOCIALIZING AGENT

A consistent theme in this passage is the fact that the respondent has guided herself through the various phases of relinquishment and transition. Glaser and Strauss (1971, p. 140) have termed this phenomenon a "solo passage" in which the person acts as her own agent of socialization, with all others playing "subsidiary roles." To varying degrees the passages of artists, entrepreneurs, and athletes such as golfers and tennis players are other examples of well-known solo passages. These passages differ from the majority of other ones which have clearly defined agents of socialization who formally control a person's passage through a sequence of roles. Teachers serve as the agents for students, doctors for patients, lawyers for clients, and so forth. In the solo passage individuals create their own timings, tactics, criteria for assessment, and learning situations. They can rely on past experience for some guidelines, but much of their socialization to roles is self-directed. This is a double-edged social situation. The absence of precedents, ground rules, timetables, and formal agents generates personal anxiety and role strain—and yet it has the benefit of allowing individuals the freedom to regulate their passage into different roles at a rate and in a manner that meets their individual needs, abilities, and desires.

When the person is her own agent in an emergent passage (as is the case for former nuns) the situation is even more complicated. Because of the emergent nature of the passage it is yet unlikely that accumulated experience can be transmitted to newcomers to forestall the pitfalls, errors, and miscalculations that inevitably accompany such movements. It is evident from the preceding pages that in emergent transitions questions of timing, direction, and control are of crucial significance in influencing the outcome of the overall passage and place a heavy responsibility on the individual who cannot rely on insitutionalized norms, stages, timetables, and strategies that make other transitions less problematic. It is better to take this job or that one? When is the right time to get one's own apartment? Is job stability or job satisfaction more important—and for whom and what? Do I date him for "the experience" or wait until someone I like comes along? Do others see me as an ex-nun or just another woman? How does one act one's age? Is it good to spend so much time with other former nuns? The "answers" to these and related questions spontaneously emerge as respondents make choices informed by past experience, present desires, commonsense knowledge, and suggestions by others.

Mistakes, miscalculations, premature moves, delays, and the like are discovered through continual reassessments and comparisons while attempts to improve one's situation generate new reference points, strategies, and choices. A respondent "realizes" that she should have left her parents' home awhile ago and begins to make plans to do so; another drops a dating partner because he "was just a learning experience" which she no longer needs; still another "comes to see" that her attitudes toward sex need to be revised in the light of recent exposure to "different types of people." The flavor of these and other illustrations indicates that the emerging transitional phase is a fluid, dynamic process of improvisation, construction and reconstruction, shifting strategies, and self-evaluation. It is edged with uncertainty, fear, and a hesitancy that is also described in other reports of emergent transitions (Atwater, 1978; Humphreys, 1972; Koffend, 1972; Skolnick, 1972).

As her own agent, the respondent underplanned the transitional phase due to the fact that it lacked the scheduled character of more institutionalized passages and formal socialization agents were generally absent.[2] At best, the plans that she made can be described as "mini-schedules" (Glaser & Strauss, 1971, p. 44), or short-term negotiations, to manage the exigencies that emerged or were created as she moved through the transition. The negotiation of first jobs, the pacing of oneself through early encounters with men, and the move from family residence to apartment are examples of these mini-schedules. More popular illustrations of this phenomenon can be found in other open-ended solo transitions, such as doctoral students who negotiate the timing of finished chapters and novelists who plan daily writing schedules.

---

[2]During the late sixties and early seventies a number of transitional agencies emerged to help former nuns and priests return to mainstream society. These agencies spontaneously arose to meet the occupational, social, and emotional needs of persons whose unique religious background presented special problems that established transitional agencies were not as able to address.

In 1971, I interviewed the director of one such agency, which had a staff composed of lay experts as well as former nuns and priests, who gave me data and personal impressions about the clientele being assisted and the range of programs and services being provided.

Basically, I learned that only a few such agencies existed throughout the country, they were often small, ad-hoc groups, and that they varied in both the range of services provided and the degree of professionalized staff that administered the programs. Many agencies relied on volunteers, had little funding, and were short-lived. Most of the clientele asked for help in finding jobs and expressed interest in the informal social gatherings that were run by these agencies.

The director's own personal impression was that there was self-selection of clientele; specifically, that former religious who made frequent use of these agencies were likely to be having more difficulty than others in making adjustments to secular life.

In discussing these agencies with respondents all were aware of their existence but only two made even one visit to ask for assistance. The general feeling of respondents was that these transitional agencies were useful primarily for former religious who were having unusual problems of adjustment. Whether or not this is true, respondents definitely preferred to use their own resources and perceived those agencies as merely an extension of convent life. They believed that seeking help from such agencies would tempt them to stay in groups and maintain relations that were part of their past. While there is no empirical evidence to support their beliefs regarding the consequences of using transitional agencies, it is significant that respondents considered the future consequences of using these agencies in terms of their impact on the passage to secular life.

Acting as their own agents, these persons are a reminder of the often neglected part individuals play in shaping social structures.

SUBSIDIARY AGENTS

Even in the solo transition, persons seek out others who can facilitate the passage to new social locations. We have seen how skillfully respondents make use of subsidiary agents to facilitate their acquisitions of social roles, selecting from a range of such persons as family members, job peers, new friends, strangers, dating partners, and former nuns. In "tenancy socialization" (Riley et al., 1972, p. 539), as contrasted with anticipatory socialization, the aim is not only to learn about role expectations, but also to engage others in reciprocal role relations and to elicit appropriate rewards for successful role performance. In emergent passages one of the problems is having to seek out for oneself, and judge the efficacy of, various potential socializing agents. Uniformed choices or poor judgment may delay passage into certain roles, cause unwanted relational problems, or produce poor articulation with other roles.

It is clear from the interview materials that subsidiary agents differ both in their *expectations* concerning appropriate behavior for persons-in-transit and in their *ability* to assist them through varying phases of transition and role acquisition. These discrepancies in expectations and abilities on the part of the socializing agents have been suggested (Bredemeier & Stephenson, 1962, pp. 111–113) as factors that retard the socialization process. In analyzing the data we have clear illustrations of this problem. In terms of differing expectations respondents report the following discrepancies: parents would pressure them to stay at home, relax, and come home early while lay friends would encourage them to do the opposite; work peers would devalue what they perceived as the respondent's overconscientiousness while friends from the convent would maintain high expectations for commitment and industriousness at work; expectations regarding data and sexual behavior contained different messages depending on whether they came from the media, the family, age peers, or former nuns.

The various agents also differed in their ability to assist in different phases of the transition as well as in different spheres of social action. Regarding spheres of action there is a clear division of labor among subsidiary agents. The family provides initial emotional support and assists in making practical adjustments to residence, budgeting, and shopping; other former nuns play more expressive roles in providing continuing emotional and psychological anchorage in addition to serving as reference groups; dating partners provide guidelines for, and affirmations of, successful performance in sex roles and romantic spheres; other agents assist in organizing information about occupational and other instrumental activities.

Agents also differed in their ability to help at different stages. In the earlier stages, soon after leaving religious life, the family, past friends, priests, and convent associates played a more vital role in assisting the respondents through initial forays into secular roles and activities. At later stages in the passage newly formed relationship were more useful. Alice Rossi's (1968, p. 29) concept, "the role cycle," is helpful here in conceptualizing the efficacy of socializing agents. She views a role as having a cycle in which each stage has its unique tasks and adjustment problems. I would now elaborate on this idea to include the fact that at different stages of a role cycle certain socializing agents may be more appropriate than others. The challenge for the individual in an emergent passage is to be sensitive to the appropriate time at which to seek new agents and to drop old ones. This dilemma is clearly illustrated in our discussion of former nuns as friends and the family members as a reference group.

Furthermore, when a person has to manage *multiple* role transitions, the complexity of this task greatly increases because the stages of the various cycles of roles one is acquiring are not likely to be at the same level of development. For example, a respondent may be much further advanced in the occupational sphere, but still be at the initial stage in the area of dating. These differential developments of multiple role cycles demand considerable sensitivity and juggling on the part of the person-in-transit in choosing appropriate agents.

TRANSITIONS AS PRECIPITATING EVENTS

Although our attention has focused on the persons who are engaged in role transitions, we should recognize the fact that when persons leave roles and move into new or different ones this activity generates problems of accommodation and role activation for others who are related to the person-in-transit. It is my belief that this is a relatively neglected area of sociological inquiry. Although we have some research on the children of a divorce, the families of prisoners, and the widow, for example, more systematic and analytical attention should be paid to the ways in which role passages set into motion various problems of accommodation for others.

Our interview data, although it gives only the respondents' side of the story, contains many references to the impact of their role exits and entrances on others. Let us look briefly at just one situation—the respondents' relation with her family. During the time that the respondent was in religious life her relations with parents and family members were segmental, regulated, and episodic in nature. Contacts were specified with regard to the frequency of visits, length of stay home, and the content of conversation regarding information about religious life. Many respondents describe their ties to their family during this time as "pleasant but superficial," "unrealistic," "stilted," or "minimal," emphasizing the point that both their role as daughters and the roles of others as parents were less salient while they were in religious life:

For sixteen years of their life (her parents) I had just never been around. I left a happy home. I was a boppin' teenager—and when I crossed that threshold there was sixteen years of their life that I hadn't been a part of. In a sense I think it was like they died for you. I had to get to know them all over again.
* * * * * *
It was seven years since I was their daughter in a real sense. We had grown apart because our lives were in separate directions. I'm not saying I forgot about them or they about me, but that we had changed and didn't know each other so well.

Once the respondents leave the convent (and especially when some go back to live with their parents) the roles of parents and daughter again become activated. But how does one respond to a daughter who left home at the age of eighteen and is now back at age thirty-three? What responsibilities does one want to assume? Which ones are resented? How will this daughter–stranger fit into the family's daily routine? What can be expected of her? Some parents, according to respondents' reports, successfully handled the reentry of their daughters into their lives with little effort:

My mother was living alone and was delighted with the company. We got along very well and she isn't the type to remind you to put on your rubbers and all that stuff—she's really very good. My mother is so independent that she lets everybody else do that.

More common, however, were complaints over the parent's perceived handling of their family roles:

It was difficult living at home because my mother still thought of me in terms of the girl who had left six years ago so it was hard for her and hard for me. The fact that I knew I was leaving to go to another city was really what kept me through in the family (sic).
* * * * * *
You are a woman and independent and for the last couple of years felt free to come and go and, now, a mother forgets this. For my mother I was still a daughter in religious life and so she became very protective and told me to watch out for this, and do that, and so all those little things my parents would do, even if they wanted to help you, would get on your nerves. I'd say "you know, I'm thirty-six years old." You have to get adjusted to that and understand that your mother wants to help you. They have to accept that you are independent and socially adjusting on your own.
* * * * * *
(Did your relations at all change with your mother when you came out?) Unfortunately they didn't change. When I came out my mother had this idea that I was her seventeen year old girl that had entered and that was out and that those seven years just hadn't done anything! I felt she treated me as a younger person and did not recognize all the responsibilities I had had in the past—that I was capable of carrying on.

At least as reported in these and other comments, the problem appears to be rooted in both age and kinship roles. The parents, and especially the mothers, seem to base their responses to their daughters in the same framework as when the teenage girls left for religious life. But these were different women now, demanding to be treated in ways that recognize this difference. In this sense, the movement of actors through role transitions in effect launches others on a passage of their own to different roles, to different arrangements within existing roles, or to the activation of latent roles and identities. The prisoner of war who returns home, the spouse who gets a divorce, the student who becomes one's colleague, and the friend who becomes one's boss are everyday examples of the way in which people inadvertently set into motion the structural movement of others. It is this story which still needs to be told by sociologists.

PASSAGE LAG

When we conceptualized role passage as a dynamic process in which persons pass through, out of, and into roles over a particular time span, we become sensitive to the fact that these movements do not occur in a unilinear, mechanical progression over fixed stages. Instead, there is considerable overlapping between phases as actors shift back and forth between past and present social locations. In analyzing the interviews it became apparent that although respondents had left the convent they continued to make some responses to present roles, situations, and persons in terms of the values and behaviors acquired in their prior roles as nuns. Reflection upon other transitions yields similar findings—the young adult who sometimes behaves as a teenager; the retired businessperson who rises early to check with the firm; the newlywed who lapses into behavior more appropriate for a single person; the novice instructor whose expectations of college students are shaped by standards applied at graduate school. I have termed this phenomenon "passage lag" and define it as the appearance in the *new* passage of specific values, self-images, preferences, and behaviors derived and carried over from the *prior* passage.[3]

Two related questions can be raised with respect to passage lag. First, to what extent does it affect the person's accommodation to present roles and to the emotional or personal vicissitudes occasioned by structural change? Second, can the relative presence or absence of such traces from past roles and identities signal the degree of adjustment persons have made to the overall transition at certain points in time? To concretize this matter and suggest

---

[3]The converse of this phenomenon has already been noted in our discussion of the nuns' anticipatory socialization, in which certain actions and responses were made in the light of their *future* roles.

possible approaches to these two issues let us look at some relevant interview materials.

The culture and social organization of the convent emphasized the primacy of the collectivity, commitment of oneself to an all-encompassing cause or calling, a devaluation of material things, hierarchical relations, and a self-effacing posture relative to others. In addition, the daily round of convent life generated a vocabulary, a set of gestures, routine modes of thought and response, and an image of oneself as a certain kind of person. That these attributes lag behind actual changes in social location is recognized by some respondents themselves, who refer to them as "hang-ups from religious life," "carry-overs," "conditioning," or "an outgrowth of the convent." Specific examples of the intrusion of prior roles in present activity are provided in the following comments:

> I miss the community we had, which I think ties up with the fact that when the year of my leave was up I didn't apply for dispensation. I wanted to find out here that sense of community and belonging that I once had in the convent.
>
> * * * * * *
>
> Our language—I think it entered every phase of your existence—religious life, that is. It really did. They taught you how to walk, how to sit, how to eat, how loud to talk—and it took with me, it took totally, and it took me a long time to extricate myself from that. People at times even now [two years later] say they sometimes can't hear me when I talk because we were always taught to speak softly. I was never relly like that; not that I was a loud-mouth or anything before [entering], but the training really got to me.
>
> * * * * * *
>
> The only thing I found difficult, and this wasn't right away either because it was too much fun at first being free, was not having a cause. I always had something that my life was centered on and that my life was focused on, and I didn't have that anymore; at least not a shared cause anyway.

Even in everyday behavior and in relations with others the former nun finds herself responding, at times, in terms of past roles. When discussing the matter of finances and their spending of money to furnish apartments, buy clothes, and make other purchases for themselves, there is an admission of guilt and a resistance to seeing oneself as "materialistic": "You're trained that material things aren't good, so you have this guilt feeling too when you buy something you really don't need." Asserting oneself is something to be learned: "At work, women would give their opinion and I felt at first that I would never think of doing that; from being in the convent you were taught to do something without thinking about it." Assuming a posture of inferiority relative to men is described by a former nun as stemming from a general orientation: "I think that bending is so much a part of us that I don't think I do it because it's a man but because it's so much a part of me now. This backing down to please was very much a part of our life in the convent." Confidence in social gatherings is hampered by prior conditioning: "I knew that I couldn't make small talk, cocktail-party talk. Again, we were always told that you don't talk—you don't make small talk—as a nun. You always talked about something, not just trivia."

Although most respondents were more sensitive to the negative consequences of passage lag for resuming secular life-styles (as the above quotations indicate), my interpretation of the data leads to positing favorable consequences as well. Especially during the early stages of the transitional period, the respondents' ability to fall back on those accustomed modes of behavior from their past helped to fill part of the structural vacuum that existed before they became more comfortable in their present secular roles. In this regard, passage lag may serve to protect persons from the unsettling consequences of not knowing how to behave or feel in new situations. However, the persistence of such elements can clearly impede the full acquisition of new roles and delay the transformation of identity.

The persistence of these traces from prior roles is also a measure of successful adjustment to new ones. Passage lag was greatest for all respondents immediately after leaving the convent. During the months and years that followed, however, passage lag was clearly related to each respondent's coming to learn and to value present roles and self-images. That is to say, the dropping of traces from past roles accompanies shifts in reference groups, role relationships, and the receiving of rewards from others for successful role performances.

In the next part of this book, we shall discuss the more complete accommodation to social roles—the final stage of the overall passage—and selected problems of multiple role passages.

PART IV

ISSUES IN MANAGING MULTIPLE ROLE PASSAGES

9
Biographical Management

Some persons, in their past or present situation, occupy roles and engage in life-styles that are defined by others as different, strange, or unacceptable. Included here are those people or behaviors that are socially stigmatized: adulterers, ex-convicts, hippies, bisexuals, the mentally ill, radicals, and the like. In the sociological literature on "deviants"—socially stigmatized persons—specific attention has been given to the acquisition of conventional social roles and life-styles by criminals (Wolfgang et al., 1962, 1970), drug and alcohol addicts (Becker, 1963; Lindesmith, 1965; Pittman, 1967; Schur, 1965), and the mentally ill (Dunham, 1965; Lefton et al., 1968; Scheff, 1967). This literature also contains sensitizing concepts, hypotheses, and theoretical formulations such as Goffman's (1963) work on stigma and information control, Scott and Lyman's (1963) typology of "accounts," the reconstruction of biography (Berger, 1963; Garfinkle, 1956, 1962, 1967), the process of stereotyping (Simmons, 1969), and the transformation of "deviant" identities (Rubington & Weinberg, 1968).

A major assumption in this body of literature is that social stigma and stereotyping impede the process of acquiring new roles and life-styles, jeopordizing the person's ability to be accepted as "normal." We are familiar, by now, with the fact that certain behaviors and individuals are the objects of stereotyping (Simmons, 1969) and, as such, are invested with the attributes of strangeness, differentness, threat, and personal stigma (Rubington & Weinberg, 1968, pp. 5–8). For persons so defined, their passage from certain roles or their acquisition of new ones raises special problems of accountability and accommodation.[1]

---

[1] See Lynn Atwater (1978) for a discussion of these problems in her analysis of women's passage to extra marital relations; also relevant is Garfinkle's (1967, pp.116–185) classic treatment of passing by an "intersexed person."

In the pilot interviews done for this research I was impressed by the frequent references made to the "stereotype of ex-nuns" and the problems it generated for former nuns who were moving into secular society. I decided, therefore, to pursue the issue with the participants in this study in order to examine the consequences of the stereotype for the negotiation of their passage.

All respondents reported that the role of nun consists of stereotypical images that color the responses of others toward them and makes it difficult for them to see themselves, and be treated by others, as "normal human beings." The following comments are illustrative of the social typing and stigmatization that surround this role:

> (Why do you say that people stereotype nuns?)
> They just treat you differently and I want to be treated normally. They're not as free with their talk. Gradually they realize that you're not going to fall apart with a swear word or about sex. It took them about a year to come to that. Some people have queer ideas about religious—some think they're homosexuals or lesbians; some think that they're just neurotic people, almost masochistic, who try to incur punishment.
> * * * * * *
> They labeled you as "nun," or "ex-nun," and then treated you as if you were that, which I wasn't really.
> * * * * * *
> I realized that there's a certain stigma to being a nun—a sense that you're strange—that there must have been something wrong with you to have become a nun in the first place; that you're abnormal. When they find out that you're an ex-nun, they treat you different. (In what way?) Oh, some of them watch their language around you, or they apologize for a sex joke, or they get very uptight when they talk to you—it's hard to explain. They did not treat you as a real person.

Goffman (1963) states succinctly the problem facing respondents:

> The stigmatized individual tends to hold the same beliefs about identity that we do. His deepest feelings about what he is may be his sense of being a "normal person," a human being like anyone else, a person, therefore, who deserves a fair break. What is desired by the individual is what can be called "acceptance." (p. 78).

The former nun wants to be treated "as a real person" yet finds that, in certain situations, the fact of being an ex-nun may preclude this from happening. The situation that respondents find themselves in, then, is one which demands that they make certain strategic choices about revealing biographical information about their past life to others; that they decide on whether or not "passing" will be an effective technique; that they accurately time biographical presentations. Goffman (1963, pp. 41–42) distinguishes two types of stigmatized persons: the discredited person, whose differentness is known to others, confronts a major task of "managing tensions generated during contacts"; the discreditable person, whose differentness is *not* known or apparent to others, confronts a major task of managing information. For the discreditable person the management of revealing information is a part of the phenomenon called "passing" and confronts persons with crucial choices: "To display or not to display; to tell or not to tell; to let on or not to let on; to lie or not to lie; and, in each case, to whom, how, when, and where."

Glaser and Strauss (1964) extend our understanding of stigma and passing by offering a paradigm for the study of awareness contexts, "the total combination of what each interactant in a situation knows about the identity of the other and his own identity in the eyes of the other" (p. 669). They distinguish four types of awareness contexts (open, closed, suspicion, and pretense) and a paradigm for studying how the structure of a social situation and the interaction of persons within that structure can shape and change the type of awareness context that exists. In the discussion that follows these contributions by Goffman and Glaser and Strauss will be used to interpret the management of stigma by former nuns as they engage in the acquisition of multiple social roles.

As sociologists have observed (Berger, 1963; Goffman, 1963), one's biography is susceptible to alteration, retrospective construction, and careful management. Information about oneself, one's past life, can be managed through various techniques so that others will remain ignorant of one's complete personal biography. For our respondents, who once were nuns, there were two questions to consider. Should they reveal to others the fact that they were once nuns? If not, how could they control this biographical information?

Let us take up the first question. At one extreme, a few respondents chose to make no effort to conceal their past role as nuns. They preferred an open awareness context (Glaser & Strauss, 1964) in which "each interactant is aware of the other's true identity and his (sic) own identity in the eyes of the other." These respondents deliberately opened the awareness context themselves by providing relevant biographical information as certain questions or situations arose:

> It really didn't make a difference to me and I felt you might as well tell them (about having been in religious life) from the beginning. It's not something I would want to hide. I'm not ashamed of having been a nun. I just told them.
> * * * * * *
> What's the point of not telling them you were a nun? If you don't, then you just have to keep telling other stories to cover it up and you can't even remember what you told different people. It is easier just to tell them.
> * * * * * *
> I always told people because it made it so uncomfortable if you didn't. (In what way?) You talk about something that happened to you and they don't understand. I'm sure some people wondered about me—wondered why I had taught all those years in the same place. As I've said before, people don't think I look young enough to be married the first time.

From these types of comments we can make two observations about the functions of revealing an accurate biography. First, to try to pass may involve oneself in what Goffman (1963, p.83) terms "in-deeper-ism," or the need to spin out more and more lies "to prevent a given disclosure." That is, the truth presented an easier strategy for some compared to the more difficult task of weaving fictitious biographical lines. Second, by telling others that one was a nun, the respondent could account for incongruous behavior and the violations of expectations as well as ward off any suspicions that others may have about who the person is in front of them. That is, having been a nun accounts for behavior and, once revealed, will make interaction more intelligible and less suspect.

Two respondents chose to pass in every situation when possible. Their motives stemmed both from a strong dislike of the differential treatment generated by stereotyping of nuns and to an equally strong unwillingness to answer the inevitable questions from persons once they learned of someone's having been in the convent:

> I didn't tell anyone. I didn't have to. I was very evasive about my past and didn't want people to know about it. I just told them I was a teacher. I used to teach at such and such a school and that I came from R. City—that's all, very evasive.
> * * * * * *
> I didn't want any questions, like "Did they really beat you?" and "Did you have to shave your head?" and all those silly remarks. I didn't want anyone to treat me other than as just me and I knew from experiences my friends had that once they find out you're an ex-nun they begin to act differently towards you.

These women maintained, in virtually all social situations, a closed awareness context (Glaser & Strauss, 1964) in which they kept from others any revealing information about their identity as ex-nuns. In this way, they attempted to minimize the interactional difficulties that they anticipated as they attempted to acquire secular roles and be accepted as "normals."

The majority of women, however, were selective in opening or keeping awareness contexts closed. Their strategies in disclosing information about themselves depended on the type of situation they were in, and the roles they were playing. They were much less likely to reveal biographical information to strangers, casual acquaintances, or work colleagues or when they were at social events such as parties, club dances, and the like. Often, they would base their decisions on the personal qualities of the other, whether or not the individual seemed tolerant, likable, and understanding. As one woman puts it, "It would depend on the person, actually. If I liked them—the type of person they were—then I would probably tell them." Through assessments of how others might respond or the possible effects of such disclosures on their ability to sustain satisfying relations with others they made ad hoc decisions to open or close the awareness context. Again we see here the reflective, active person-in-passage who takes control over problematic issues with a sensitivity to the consequences of her actions for smooth relationships and acceptable identities.

The disclosure of information and the managing of awareness contexts are processual, developmental phenomena in which persons, or the structure of the situation itself, produce deliberate or inadvertent changes in the awareness context. This is evident when we consider the temporal management of selective biographies by our respondents. Through trial and error experiences these women developed certain rules of thumb for the proper timing of biographical disclosures.

The "proper time" for disclosures was dependent on the situation or role relation the respondent confronted. For example, at least with their first employment positions, these respondents were candid with employers during job interviews about having once been in religious life.[2] With dating partners the biographical strategies differed. Some women were adamant about immediate disclosure, perhaps, as suggested earlier, to smooth the passage to romantic and sexual relations. Others, however, preferred a wait-and-see posture, in order to determine whether or not the relationship was likely to continue for more than a brief period of time. In general, respondents preferred to postpone biographical facts until after the relationships had some time to develop:

> I usually prefer that that's not the first thing people know about me because I think it does color their perception of you. I'd rather not tell them until they get to know me first.
>
> * * * * * *
>
> I would tell people after I got to know them better because I was wondering what their reaction would be, and wanted them to accept me for what I was now. I was afraid that they wouldn't react to me in the same way if first they knew I had been in the convent.

In fact, this decision to postpone biographical information was due to negative reactions to early disclosures. One woman discusses an initial reaction to opening the awareness context which made her rethink her strategy for timing a disclosure:

> On one of the first dates I had I told the guy right off that I had been a nun and you should have seen his reaction. He stopped the car, pulled over and leaned back and said, "Oh my God! A nun! I don't believe it. What am I supposed to do? Nobody will believe I took out a nun!" It was a real scene, and he was very uncomfortable, so after that I decided to wait at least until he had got to know me better.

---

[2]Their candor may have been determined, to a large extent, by the fact that job applications require either an employment history (including prior positions, salaries, references) or an explanation of the absence of such a history. In this regard, an open awareness context in occupational roles is structured into the situation itself.

One problem, of course, with postponing such information is the possibility of feeling that one has not reciprocated an exchange of confidence and trust with the other and of damaging the relationship by any further delay. Caught in this bind a respondent states:

> It got to the point where I really had to tell her—I felt I was being dishonest and I wanted her to know this part of me. I wondered if she would be angry when she found out, but she wasn't. I was glad to have it out in the open.

In commenting on this possible situation Goffman (1963) observes that:

> Every relationship obliges the related persons to exchange an appropriate amount of intimate facts about self, as evidence of trust and mutual commitment. Newly formed or "post-stigma" relationships are very likely to carry the discreditable person past the point where he feels it has been honorable of him to withhold the facts.   (p.86)

Both premature and delayed disclosures can threaten the successful acquisition of valued roles and relationships. One may open an awareness context too early and thus incur interactional problems based on responses to stereotypes and stigma, as illustrated in the quotation regarding early disclosure to dating partners. On the other hand, delayed disclosures may also generate strain in relationships, since others expect authenticity in how we present ourselves to them. With practice and conscious reflection, most respondents learned to devise appropriate temporal strategies for disclosure, but until they did, they confronted a variety of barriers to successful adjustment.

What were some of the techniques used by former nuns to manage biographical information about themselves? The most frequently used technique to conceal signs of their past role as nuns was the manipulation of physical appearance. There is a belief on the part of former nuns (as well as in some sectors of the Catholic community) that through their appearance, gestures, and clothes some women look like "ex-nuns." This stereotype contains some of the following elements: "dowdy, frumpy clothes," "conservative dress," "an old-fashioned hairdo," "little or no jewelry," "no makeup," "short hair that is not styled," "restricted movements," "a quiet manner," and being "uncomfortable with her body." By managing her physical presentation, then, the respondent not only was working to present herself as a woman but also to prevent others from typecasting her as an "ex-nun." As one woman put it, "I didn't want everybody to say,'Oh, she's one of those!' when they looked at me. I didn't want to look like an ex-nun."

The symbolic meaning of clothing, accessories, physique, and other physical presentations was recognized by every respondent as a set of cues to their prior roles as nuns. Each woman went to some lengths to camouflage her religious past and her present role as "ex-nun." They wanted to present a self that would not be suspect, especially in routine, day-to-day life. Interestingly, this was true even for those women who chose early disclosure as their preferred strategy. A perceptive respondent highlights the part played by physical presentations in controlling biographical information:

> I didn't want to look like I was uncomfortable in my role as a lay person, and now when I look back on it, it's not just the clothing itself, but the way a person wears the clothes, how they enter the room and how they sit down that really says whether they are comfortable or not.

As Stone (1962, pp.86–118) notes, the self is presented in a variety of ways and appearances are sources of crucial information about one's various identities. By altering one's physical presentation one could control telling information about one's identity. As another respondent observes, "I didn't want my looks to give away my past."

Other techniques for controlling awareness contexts included the giving of misinformation, evasive tactics, silence, and control over one's behavior. This range of information control is evident in the following remarks by four respondents:

> Whenever a question arose about where I worked in my last job I would just say that it was in a small school in a nearby State, which I knew nobody would have heard of.
>
> * * * * * *
>
> If the topic of dating would come up I would be very general and just try to say very little about it—I would just listen.
>
> * * * * * *
>
> As soon as the talk got personal I would change the subject. I tried to steer away from questions about my personal life.
>
> * * * * * *
>
> You know, ex-nuns are known to be very quiet and polite and reserved and in not wanting to fall into that stereotype I tried to be more outgoing, more forward.

Although respondents were frequently successful at passing, there were other situations in which biographical information was difficult or impossible to manage and the respondent moved from discreditable to discredited. Seen from another perspective, the structure of certain situations forced closed contexts to become open, independently of the person's own wishes in the matter. These "contingencies in passing" (Goffman, 1963, pp.75–86) remind us that there are limits to the role player's ability to steer her passage exactly as she would prefer.

The most frequent instances of a passing contingency which opened the awareness context occurred in the occupational sphere. Information required on job applications or sought during the job interview made it difficult to conceal one's past religious affiliations:

> I told them I was in religious life because they could tell by looking at the application. "Where did you teach?" "All Catholic schools." "What was your salary?" "Nothing." "Where did you live last?" "At a convent."
>
> * * * * * *
>
> If you just say that you've been teaching for ten years, they would want to know where. If you say you taught at three Catholic schools for three years each, they look kinda funny. Like, I was in for years and you can't avoid telling it.
>
> * * * * * *
>
> At some point you're asked what organizations you belong to, where you've traveled, what hobbies you have and this plus the other information, like no salary, just makes it impossible not to tell them.

Once such information was obtained by employers it seemed highly likely that it would move through the occupational grapevine and become known to one's work colleagues:

> At the hospital the word just spread like wildfire. This girl whose job I took had a big mouth and she told just about everyone there. I realized this afterwards— that everybody in that hospital knew I was a nun.
>
> * * * * * *
>
> The first day I went to work the other two counselors were all uptight over this— a nun coming to work with them! They told me this since. "An ex-nun coming to work!" (How did they know you were an ex-nun?) I don't know. This is what I'm saying: why try to hide it because it gets all over the place anyway.

Passing is always endangered when one confronts a person who knew you in your prior role. On occasion, respondents would encounter neighbors, former classmates, students, and parishioners whose personal identification of them threatened their cover. In a related vein, persons who had such prior knowledge (family, neighbors, relatives, and friends) sometimes would make this information known to others.

Two additional contingencies were also uncovered in the interviews and they underscore the need, by those who pass, "to be alive to aspects of the social situation which others treat as uncalculated and unattended" (Goffman, 1963, p.88). Failure to do so can result in an embarrassing incident, a faux pas, or other event that casts suspicion on one's present identity claims. A respondent recalled visiting at the apartment of another former nun and waiting for almost an hour before being offered a drink and comments:

> I felt that this poor girl didn't quite have the hang of socializing yet and entertaining. That's the kind of thing you don't learn in fifteen years. You never played hostess in that style, doing those sorts of things. It's those tiny things that embarrass you and give you away.

Another former nun described an incident in which her response to a stranger inadvertently called her into question:

Just getting on a bus the other day someone had asked me for directions and I told them. The bus driver said, "Are you a Sister?" I was surprised, because I was dressed very casually—even chewing gum—and I thought I was so cool, part of the scene, and I asked him why he said that, and he said,"It's your whole manner with that woman. People just don't do that. It's rare." I told him I was in the convent.

The following incident is an example of a multiple contingency encounterd by still another former nun who was attempting to pass:

One time she said that she bowls on the night I went to school and asked if I would like to drop by after classes. So I did, and all of a sudden I looked up and said, "When did they put up these electric scoreboards?" She just looked at me as if to say, "Where have you been?" and I thought, "Oh, my God. What did I do?" Then the husband of one of these women came over and said, "Don't I know you? You look so familiar?" Well, I had been to college with him when I was in the convent. I said, "Yes, you know me." "How do I know you?" I said, "I was in a class with you at college." He said, "Oh, my God!" Then he didn't say anything else. I winked, you know, and he made the connection. So finally, the next day at school this girl came to my office and said, "What's going on? What's this mystery about you?" So I told her, and she was so aghast she didn't believe it at all.

This quote illustrates the other two awareness contexts suggested by Glaser and Strauss (1964). The suspicion context occurs when one partner suspects the true identity of the other, in this case the respondent's co-workers. The pretense context occurs when both interactants are fully aware of the other's identity "but pretend not to be," in this case the man in the above incident. This event vividly illustrates the fragile nature of awareness contexts and how they can change in a brief social encounter. It also underscores the delicate balance of control over awareness contexts that shifts from role player to role partners.

Finally, it is part of the commonsense understanding of a person's biography that it will normally contain a range of events, behavior, and role relationships that make up the usual round of life experience for many people. When respondents first left religious life, they were acutely aware of this gap in their biographical line and often found that it precipitated the need to disclose their past identity as nuns:

They would ask you what you did for the last twenty years. You had no frame of reference for talking about things, and for your social life. So, finally, I just had to say that I'd been in the convent, period. You had to account for your past someway, and then things in your past just took their rightful place.

* * * * * *

Usually it would come up when people got in questions as to what you've been doing with your life. I know that right after I left it was very hard. If you weren't going to tell them that you were in the convent there was no frame of reference for anything. Now it isn't necessary, but at first it was almost impossible not to tell them you were in the convent because you had no frame of reference. There was nothing that you could discuss because you had no shared experiences with those outside.

Respondents, at first, were at a loss in coming up with biographical accounts that could be shared with others, or at least that others were familiar with. Those years in religious life, if they were to be concealed, meant that one had to fill in a considerable block of time. "You had no common experiences with others unless you made them up," as one former nun remembers. These biographical gaps made respondents acutely aware of their differentness and was a source of interactional strain that could be resolved only by disclosure or the weaving of a fictitious biographical line.

In examining the strategies of biographical management by former nuns who had been out of the convent for different lengths of time, we discovered that there is a shift in their biographical presentations and problems. On the one hand, as the respondent becomes more confident in her ability to move into secular life and successfully play a variety of roles she is less hesitant than before to reveal her past religious role. She may now have her own apartment, have new friends, have traveled, have a satisfying job. These acquisitions of roles and experiences are evidence to herself and to others that she is more than "ex-nun," that she is like everyone else. A respondent who was out for four years describes this change:

After a year or two I felt more secure in myself and now I don't mind telling people. (More secure?) In their reaction to me and more secure in my own position. I don't feel as defensive as I used to; I know I can make it; I am more certain of myself now.

As the former nun takes her place in secular society, as two, three, and more years pass from the time she left the convent, she builds up a repertoire of roles and experiences that will offset the possibly negative reactions to her disclosure. In addition, the significance of having been a nun declines in importance. Another respondent, who had been out for three years, confides that after a year or so "you start forgetting a lot of your past yourself and it's not that important anymore. Having been a nun is increasingly less important to me and that too may be the reason why I don't care now if people know." Respondents who had been out of the convent for longer periods of time were less likely than those out more recently to avoid disclosure or try to pass. For them, the role of ex-nun becomes less salient as they take on additional identities and roles.

If, in the passing of time, these acquisitions reduce the desire or the need to pass or control biographical information, they serve the paradoxical function of facilitating passing. As stated earlier, the majority of respondents did prefer to pass with strangers, casual associates, and the like. By having accumulated an acceptable biographical line in the early postconvent years, respondents could now fall back on these experiences without having to mention the convent or to get involved in the arduous task of fabrication. This flexibility is expressed quite clearly:

> I'm not pressured into telling somebody now because it's three years later and I've got some background. Like I had had these other three jobs so I can say I had these other jobs and don't even go into the teaching bit (when she was a nun) sometimes. I've just got some background of being out now.
> * * * * * *
> I don't feel any need to tell others now because I have a variety of job experiences. I've traveled; I've acquired other things that I can share with people—similar experiences and stuff.
> * * * * * *
> Earlier, when people asked you what you were doing, where you've been, who you were, I didn't have anything to tell them except to tell them about the convent. Now, I feel I have had enough exposure, I have done enough things to be able to fill in those answers without having to mention the convent if I didn't want to.

Thus by accumulating an acceptable range of postconvent experiences the respondent who had been out a longer period of time found it easier to manage passing contingencies, to have options for disclosing, and to validate her claim to being someone other than just an "ex-nun."

While the theoretical issues and ideas that frame this chapter are usually employed in studies of behavior that is highly stigmatized, such as serious crime, addiction, or homosexuality, I believe their usefulness in analyzing other sociological questions has been demonstrated and should be encouraged. As the case of former nuns implies, the fact that one is different than others, even when this difference does not yield a strong, primarily *negative* stereotype, raises problems of biographical management and makes role passage problematic. The returning POW, the child prodigy, and the instant millionaire also can be studied from this perspective.

Furthermore, questions of biographical management should become increasingly central to studies of emergent passages themselves because they involve modifications of established roles or the pathways to these roles. Many of these passages are likely to meet with some resistance, fear, or suspicion, as has been the case for men who choose vasectomies, couples living in "open marriage," vegetarians, and other social inventors. The empirical investigation of how they manage awareness contexts and biographical presentations should yield generous sociological benefits.

10
Priority and Linkage

When persons are confronted with the task of managing not just one but a number of transitions at the same time, the questions of priority and linkage take on increasing practical and theoretical importance. By priority we mean simply the relative ranking of roles and role-related tasks in terms of more or less importance in demanding attention and action on the part of the person-in-passage. We are assuming here that an individual cannot devote equal amounts of energy, attention, and activity to all roles simultaneously and will have to set up, at least temporarily, some list of priorities to guide her allocation of personal resources. Linkage, or articulation, refers to the goodness of fit or correspondence between two or more roles. We are aware that roles can be mutually supportive or highly competitive with one another; that structural expectations may coincide or conflict with each other.[1] How respondents handle these problems of priority and linkage is the focus of this chapter.

Let us first take up the question of priorities. Of the many roles respondents were resuming or acquiring and the multiplicity of activities they were engaging in, there emerges a rather clear, broad ordering of priorities for virtually all respondents. Basically, matters of residence and family were first, followed by occupational attainment and the management of personal

---

[1]These two issues have received a good deal of attention in the sociological literature. Two widely known treatments are Merton's (1968, pp.425–433) identification of the social mechanisms that articulate roles in the role set, and Goode's (1960) theory of role strain. A more thorough development of the problems of priority and linkage is provided in Glaser and Strauss' (1971, pp.142–156) analysis of multiple passages.

appearance, with socializing, dating, and joining new groups coming last. This ranking of roles and activities reflects, first, that practical expediency plays a large part in shaping initial priorities and, second, that respondents were sensitive to the manner in which successful movement into subsequent roles is contingent upon adequately managing prior ones. This rank ordering also closely approximates the respondents' feelings of ease and control over various spheres of life; that is, they engaged in activities over which they had greater familiarity and control, such as residence or personal appearance. They also ordered priorities in terms of the degree to which roles and activities were emotionally or socially threatening, such as postponing dating, sexual activity, and the joining of groups until later stages of passage.

Although this gross ordering obtained, unforeseen events served to alter the priorities for certain respondents—a family illness caused one woman to temporarily put aside social activities; a failure to find employment delayed another woman's adjustment to family life and residence. As Glaser and Strauss (1971) observe, such critical events "tend to 'flood' the lives of the pasagee so that virtually all other passages may have to be temporarily 'frozen' or even permanently abandoned" (p.144). In other instances, unexpected and positive events precipitated a reordering of priorities, as when one respondent got engaged after having been out less than a year, or another resumed a past friendship that immediately brought her into a circle of new acquaintances and dating partners. In these cases respondents had to shift tactics, juggle time, postpone other activities and reallocate resources as unanticipated events, both desirable and unwanted, "flooded" their lives.

Periodic assessment of priorities were also made. Respondents would shift the relative ordering of priorities when they felt that satisfactory adjustments were being made in certain spheres or that more attention had to be devoted to other areas. For example, once respondents felt that their physical appearance and wardrobe were adequate, they shifted their attention and energies to other activities, such as meeting new people or reconsidering their residential location. This continual reordering of priorities over time reflects the shifts in respondents' "identities as well as interests" (Glaser & Strauss, 1971, p.149) and highlights the problem of articulating the various passages in the transition.

When we consider that these women were making a dramatic change in life-style that entailed accommodations to work, sex, and age roles, social life, and family, it is evident that the ease with which the transition is made will depend on the successful linkages among these multiple roles. The most ideal situation for persons-in-passage would be one in which (1) the expectations of different roles complemented one another or were well integrated; (2) the role player would have the capability to behave in ways that minimize conflicting role demands; (3) the signals or cues of inadequate linkage were clear and immediately evident; and (4) the social environment, including events and other role players, was benign or fortuitous. But social life for role players is seldom ideal. For example, respondents found that while certain roles supported one another other roles were more likely to place conflicting demands on the former nun's resources. Occupational roles, for instance, could not only provide the financial means to implement changes in the respondent's personal situation (buying clothes, financing a car, paying the rent) but also served as an opportunity to expand one's circle of associates and to encounter role models for age and sex behavior. Maintaining exclusive ties to other former nuns, however, delayed the acquisition of new relationships and exposure to events that were based in the present and necessary for the development of new self-imagery. Further, as some respondents discovered, roles that were supportive at one time became competitive at a later date. A case in point is the shift in family relations from one that was emotionally and financially supportive to one that was later perceived as an impediment to autonomy and maturation.

Respondents also differed in their ability to meet the challenge of role articulation, some being better able than others to behave in ways that forged supportive links between roles. We have already indicated how some women made decisions and formulated particular strategies to effectively link certain passages to one another. They changed jobs, residence, physical appearance, friends, dating partners, and biographies when they perceived these alterations as working to improve the links between roles. The proper timing of these moves was important to forestall unforeseen consequences that would adversely affect other passages, and some respondents were better able than others to make these decisions and make them at the right time. For example, one woman made a premature job change that threatened her financial security, and another made an overdue break with past friends that left her without a partner for ventures into social life. These, and other instances of premature and delayed choices, underscore the fact that the demands of linkage are not equally within the range of every role player's capabilities.

It is a basic sociological axiom that role players who experienced the structurally induced strain of poorly articulated roles will attempt to reduce that strain by employing one or more strategies of action (Goode, 1960; Merton, 1968). What should be emphasized here is that taking action to reduce role strain depends on possessing a certain understanding of oneself as a role player and one's connection to the social structure. Put simply, persons need to possess what C. Wright Mills (1959) termed "the sociological imagination," the awareness of the critical connection between their private experience and the structure and processes of social life. The signs of poorly articulated roles, the cues to role strain, are often ambiguous or subtle in the first place. We may sense that "something is wrong" with our circle of friends, with our jobs, or family relations but we may not be able to pinpoint the difficulty. Even if we can, if we lack a sociological imagination, we may define the strain as stemming from personal inadequacies, bad luck, or sources other than structural ones.

Some respondents, for example, were acutely sensitive to the link between their "private troubles" as women, workers, family members, and friends and the structural sources of their difficulties in these roles. Other women were more likely to explain their present situation in psychological or individualized terms:

> (Why do you think other ex-nuns are having "better luck" at dating?) Because, as I told you, I think they are just different personalities, they are more flexible, they just don't find as many faults with men and the whole dating scene that I do. It's just an individual matter really.
>
> * * * * * *
>
> I see other ex-nuns who just fit into their family and jobs with ease and I suppose I'm the one with the hang-ups. They seem better adjusted psychologically and they just try harder to make the best of things.

As long as these respondents define their present situations in highly personalized or individualized ways I doubt that they can as effectively behave in ways that would bring their roles into better integration with one another.

A related issue concerns the fact that although persons may correctly define strain as coming from disarticulated roles, they may not feel able to do whatever it requires to alleviate the situation. For example, one respondent insisted she was "not the type to live alone" although she strongly felt that living with her parents was a hindrance to her social life. Another former nun indicated that it took her many months to seek another job with a better salary because she "didn't have the guts to face another interview." Still another woman understood the social limitations of her exclusive ties to other former nuns but she "couldn't stop seeing them so much because it makes me feel guilty and selfish." While these perceptions of one's abilities may validly be conceptualized as psychological matters, as sociologists we can understand them with equal validity as exercises in "bad faith"; that is, "to pretend something is necessary that in fact is voluntary" (Berger, 1963, p.143). To be in "bad faith" is to refuse to see that we can, as role players, make choices as to how we play out our roles, that we are not just bundles of psychological predispositions or solely bound by role expectations. While it is not my intention here to go into the societal sources of "bad faith" and the failure to view our lives with "a sociological imagination" I want to emphasize the part they play in effecting the decisions role players make in articulating role passages, and thus, by extension, the kind of adjustment which is made to these passages.

Although there is a continual need for all role players to articulate their passage through various stages in the life course, this process is somewhat unique for our respondents. Because of the unstructured nature of the transition, respondents must rely more fully on their own resources to develop strategies, forge links, create timetables, and make the choices that will reduce the strains of disarticulated roles. When persons are in more institutionalized passages, they can rely to a larger degree on the existence of norms, schedules, ceremonies, and established priorities to facilitate articulation. While this does not mean that in institutionalized passages problems of articulation will not arise, we want to stress that in emergent transitions the process and problems of articulation are more primary and more difficult to negotiate.

While there are costs involved in having to forge these links more or less on one's own, there are also rewards. Moving outside the boundaries of traditional roles, bypassing conventional pathways to these social locations, and occupying unexpected combinations of roles are also liberating social experiences. Accompanying the confusion and fear that these actions involve is also a sense of personal freedom and authenticity. The lives of those on the frontier of social existence are a mixture of both the dark and light sides of being different.

Finally, as our institutionalized ways of living need to be reordered and rearranged, demanding new priorities and new linkages between roles, the study of these kinds of passages becomes a more central challenge for sociology.

11

Validation of Role Acquisitions

In the last two chapters we investigated the respondents' management of biographical presentations and their efforts to articulate multiple role acquisitions. These activities should be understood as an integral part of the process of acquiring roles and the social identities that flow from them. In this chapter we will complete our discussion of this third stage of role passage by examining the question of role validation.

The successful acquisition of social roles requires both personal and social validation. The task at hand is to inquire into this process of validation: how does the person-in-transit know the extent to which she has successfully passed through stages of her passage? how does she measure her adjustment? what personal and social cues does she use? what part do others play in validating her acquisition of roles and identities? For analytical purposes we shall separate the discussion of personal and social validation while nonetheless recognizing their interdependence in actual social life.

PERSONAL VALIDATION

A major sociological axiom states that people's self-image and personality is, in part, influenced by the roles they play and the groups they belong to. Anselm Strauss (1962) effectively captures this idea in his remark that a role "is likely to become a way of being as well as a way of acting" (p.79). As role players, individuals come to identify themselves with their roles and incorporate into their personality dimensions of these social locations. We should expect, then, that as former nuns become involved in passages to differernt roles and groups their image of themselves, their self-understandings, and their personality will also undergo changes that reflect these acquisitions.

In a pointed and thoughtful discussion, Clausen (1972) asserts that "to a very considerable degree personality is anchored in the primary group memberships and major role commitments of the individual. Let these change significantly and the person will change" (p.501). If former nuns have, indeed, shifted their major group memberships and roles, then they should have different assessments and images of themselves. We should also recall our definition of successful adjustment to role passage as one in which respondents come to define themselves in new terms, to possess images of themselves that are grounded in present or future roles. As sociologists, we would expect respondents, as they accommodate themselves to role changes, to report changes in their personality and self-image.[1]

Every respondent indicated that, as a result of being in a secular world, she had in fact experienced some change within herself. The most frequently mentioned alterations were a sense that she was "more herself" now that she was out of the confines of the religious roles; that she was responding to herself and to others in a more "genuine" way, reflecting her own feelings, needs, desires, and aspirations rather than those dictated by a social role. A very characteristic illustration of this reaction is reflected in the following remark:

> I have become a person—me! There's no role to play, like you had to when you were a nun. I can be me, not what someone at the Motherhouse expects me to be. People now respond to me, not the role of Sister.

From a sociological perspective it is ironic that while respondents reported a sense of freedom from the role demands of being a nun they did not recognize the secular role demands that were in fact shaping their lives as adults, as women, as workers, as citizens, and so forth. My interpretation of this phenomenon is that *by comparison* the role of nun is more encompassing in its demands than many secular roles they were playing, which led them to believe they were not responding as role players but just "as me." Most respondents were quite insistent that they were now behaving in a more "authentic" way, in a manner that reflected their unique personality and not merely the external demands of a social role. To this extent, all respondents indicated that changing social roles produced some change in their understanding of themselves and their response to others.

Additionally, most respondents were adamant in reporting a greater sense of independence in learning to think for themselves, to make their own

---

[1]While it is true that not everyone who changes roles will be equally adept at recognizing and reporting the concomitant changes in personality and self-image, the dramatic and emerging nature of the changes made by former nuns, plus their own skills as reflective respondents, gives us confidence in their estimates of personal change.

choices, and to take responsibility for their lives. The overall impression one gets from the interview data is a reported change in the direction of increased personal and social maturity. They spoke enthusiastically of greater confidence in their individual abilities, a desire to take control of their lives, a willingness to take risks, and an increasing capacity to look to themselves for self-approval.

In order to determine if respondents' assessments of the degree of personal change was related to their actual adjustment to secular roles and life-styles I categorized respondents on a broad continuum of role acquisition. At one end of the continuum I placed those ten respondents who, based on the interview data, had made the most successful adjustment to their passage as we have defined this term in our study. These respondents had made lay friends, found their jobs satisfactory, established their own residences, were engaged, married, or reported satisfaction with their social life, and, generally, had experienced a range of secular activities such as traveling, joining organizations, pursuing hobbies, etc.

The following comments from some of these respondents reveal a substantial change in their identity and personality:

> It wasn't until last December that I felt I had made the transition. It wasn't until then that I felt I was no longer trying to catch up; no longer trying to prove myself; no longer trying to duplicate the achievements of others or worrying about socializing and all that.
>
> * * * * * *
>
> I have different friends, I am good at work, I have my own apartment—I'm a new person. It took me two years to build up a new life for myself but I think I've done it.
>
> * * * * * *
>
> I think in the beginning you're conscious of being an ex-nun. The more people tell you, "My God! You're not an ex-nun." Or, "You don't look like one," the more you begin to believe that, so the less you're conscious about or worried about it. I think that if you're not happy out here and you're more oriented to the past you will be more conscious of being an ex-nun and look back at the times when you were happy as a nun. If you make a good adjustment, whatever a good adjustment is, and are really happy with yourself you're less likely to think of yourself as an ex-nun. Just like back to looks. If I couldn't believe that I didn't look like an ex-nun then I'd constantly be thinking of myself as an ex-nun and I couldn't get away from that.
>
> * * * * * *
>
> I am more future-oriented now, or present-oriented now, instead of past-oriented. I have completely closed and locked the door on the convent. It is over. It is in the past.

These respondents have successfully integrated the convent experience into their present life situation. They are concerned about the present and the future; they see themselves in terms of ongoing relations and affiliations. They no longer define themselves as "ex-nuns" and they express confidence in their secular life-style.

At the other end of the continuum were four respondents who, in most areas of social life, had made few accommodations to secular society. They were either unemployed or unsatisfied in their jobs, they had not made new friends or changed the base of their prior friendships, they were not pursuing, or pursuing successfully, intimate relations with others, they were financially and emotionally dependent on their families—in sum, they were in, but not of, secular society. These respondents did not report substantial changes in self-image and personality:

> Even after a year and a half it's (the convent) so much a part of me, where a lot of other people have kind of shrugged it right off so it's a part of their life but it's past, you know? I'll probably never go back (into the convent), but it's still a part of me.
>
> * * * * * *
>
> I think about it. I just feel it's still with me. Those fourteen years—the good and the bad—are a very important part of my life and I don't think I'll ever be able to completely put it behind me.
>
> * * * * * *
>
> I don't feel I've changed very much since I've left. I guess that because I haven't been able, yet, to substitute other things for what I had in the convent. I know I should make new friends; I would like to be dating; I want to do a lot of things, but I think I lack the confidence.

Here we note the failure to integrate the prior experiences of religious life into present personal and social life. Being a nun and having been in the convent are still important reference points for self-image and personality.

In the midpoint of the continuum were six respondents who were in the transitional stages of the overall passage, having made accommodations in some roles and activitites but not in others. Their images of themselves were contingent upon the kinds of accommodations they had or had not made. One respondent, whose dating life was meager, said she was "still not very confident in myself as a woman—that I'm attractive to men"; another, who just recently acquired a professional position, remarked that "maybe now I can build up my confidence and respect for myself as a professional person"; still another respondent, whose close friends were mostly other former nuns, reflected on the fact that "maybe if my friends were different, if I make new friends, I wouldn't be so conscious of being an ex-nun." Living at home with her parents produced this response from a thirty-year-old respondent:

> I think that if I was living in my own apartment I would feel better about myself as an adult, as a successful person who may have once been a nun but is now just an average person. It's hard to really feel different about yourself otherwise. That's why I'm thinking of moving out soon. Ex-nuns still live at home.

In sum, successful accommodations to role passage are reflected in changing definitions of oneself, in the characteristics we attribute to ourselves, and in our evaluations of the kinds of persons we are or have become. In this sense, role passages are occasions for self-transformation; they are structural moves that affect how we know ourselves.

SOCIAL VALIDATION

Although we have found that changes in self-imagery reflect changes in structural positions, we must also inquire as to the part played by others in allocating persons to new social roles. Riley et al. (1972) correctly argue that while role relinquishment does not usually require the approval or validation of others, "role assumption is not merely a decision made by the candidate himself. It requires, also, acceptance and validation by some *others*" (p. 559). One can only come to see herself in a role if some other accords her that existence by making the appropriate *reciprocal* responses of a related role. To see oneself, for example, as a friend, lover, professional, woman, or adult one must elicit responses from others that certify one's claim to be these kinds of people. In this regard, we can understand many of the postconvent behaviors, choices, and negotiations of these respondents as strategies for getting others to define and respond to them not as ex-nuns but as occupants of other social positions.

The following comments illustrate the way in which others allocate and confirm a person's role acquisitions and corresponding self-definition:

(Are you saying that people's reactions to you make you more or less conscious of being an ex-nun?) Yes. We were down at a convention and some nuns were ahead of us on the boardwalk and one of my co-workers said to me, "Oh, look. Do you know them?" and I said, "No," and she said, "They're looking at you," and I said, "They're probably saying, "Ah-hah! She's a runaway—renegade," and she said to me, "They'd never think you were," and I knew what she was saying. She meant that other people don't think of me as an ex-nun; that I don't get that kind of reaction from them.

* * * * * *

I would say that although I knew I was a woman, I didn't feel that other people knew, but now I don't feel that way. (Why?) Because now people define you as a woman—they treat you like a woman.

* * * * * *

You know what makes you begin to forget that you're an ex-nun? People. It's people's responses to you. They begin to act towards you differently, like a woman, a girlfriend, a person at work. It takes a while for that to happen, of course, but when it does it's sort of like a confirmation of the fact that you've made it.

In order to validate one's claim to be more than an ex-nun, to feel successfully adjusted to secular roles these women had to gain the appropriate responses from others who were their role partners. Validation by others, in turn, was dependent on the following variables: the amount of anticipatory socialization respondents had engaged in; the length of time available to them for role-learning and role practice (Mann & Mann, 1959); the opportunities for, and their ability to select, proper subsidiary agents; and their success at biographical management and role linkage. To the degree that respondents differed according to these variables they were differentially successful in getting others to validate their acquisition of social roles.

The issue of social validation is of special importance in studying emergent passages because it is more problematic for the person-in-passage than for those going through institutionalized passages. As Glaser and Strauss (1971, pp. 41-42) note, "closure ceremonies" abound in more institutionalized passages to signal the successful completion of a structural journey. These ceremonies and rituals function to validate the claims of the person-in-passage to having accomplished the passage; closure ceremonies also call to the attention of others that a new kind of person is in front of them who should be responded to in different ways. Popular examples of ritualized closure include graduation day exercises, birth announcements, weddings, military induction ceremonies, and bar mitzvah. By contrast, emergent passages are devoid of such ceremonial validation.[2] How do persons in such passages come to recognize if and when they have completed their journey? In the absence of ritualized closure what cues do they seek to signal their accommodation to different roles and identities and how much confidence do they express in their judgments?

I pursued this question with respondents and have come to a few initial conclusions. First, respondents expressed considerable confidence in knowing the extent to which they had fully accommodated themselves to secular life. Their reactions ranged from "I've made it completely back into the world," through "I'm almost there," to "I still have a ways to go." They were able to recognize variations in degree of passage completion and to place themselves with confidence along a continuum of accomplishment.

Second, not only were they confident about their placement they were also fairly accurate if my own judgment as an outsider is used as a measure of their accommodation. I located each respondent at varying points in the passage according to the composition of her role set, her range of secular experiences, and her source of self-image. With two exceptions, where the respondents' and my own evaluation were different, there was consensus as to the degree to which respondents had completed their passage.

---

[2]Emergent passages are not the only ones lacking ceremonial validation. In many passages out of stigmatized roles there is also a lack of ceremony to symbolize the passage to conventional society. Prisoners, patients in mental hospitals, and former drug and alcohol addicts are just a few of the persons whose reentry is seldom signified and celebrated by ceremonial validation.

Third, respondents were aware of social cues and used them as criteria to assess their adjustment. Although they did mention, as signals of their relative adjustment, such psychological attributes as "being happy," "feeling confident," or "liking myself," they made more frequent use of role-related criteria. They specifically mentioned activities or relationships that are grounded in social roles: "having new friends," "dating men," "financial independence," "a good job," etc. We can infer from these findings that, even in the absence of ceremonial validation, persons can generate or find criteria for measuring passage completion, that they can develop confidence in their estimations, and that they give a prominent place to role-related criteria in making their assessments.

One last point will close this chapter. I have presented a dual measure of the extent to which persons-in-passage are accommodating themselves to different roles and life-styles. One is psychological, and refers to self-imagery, while the other is sociological, and refers to the allocation by others to social roles. Both work to validate claims to points on a journey through roles. These two measures are conceptually interrelated and experientially interdependent. Insofar as persons receive role validating responses from others they are encouraged to embrace certain images of themselves. These self-images, in turn, increase the likelihood that role behavior appropriate to one's self-conceptions will follow, thus eliciting further role validation from others. This dynamic cycle of personal and social validation is at the heart of all negotiated passages.

PART V
CONCLUSION

12

Some Implications of Emergent Role Passage for Sociology

One of the primary goals of exploratory research is to return to one's conceptual model with suggestions for revisions, specifications, additions, and confirmations derived from one's research findings. In this chapter we return to our initial conceptualization of role passage and see how the present study may serve to inform and elaborate our theoretical model.

Before we move to a summary examination of the revised model, let us briefly reiterate what we believe to be some of the special configurations of this study. First, this is an *emergent* passage, being shaped and controlled by the person as she goes through the transition rather than being formed by institutionalized rules, timetables, choices, and meanings. In their formal theory of status passage, Glaser and Strauss (1971, pp. 85–86) make but a brief reference to the emergent passage. They characterize it as one that is created, discovered, and shaped by the parties as they go along. By its very nature, the emergent passage is an open-ended, improvised, innovative one that may, over time, become institutionalized. We have proposed a more specific definition of the emergent passage as one in which persons either create new roles or modify the institutionalized pathways of existing ones. The explicit and primary theoretical focus of this study is the exploration of emergent role passage.

Second, we have concentrated on a passage through *multiple* roles thus forcing our attention to the problems of priority and articulation among roles. The focus on multiple, as opposed to single, role passage more closely approximates the actual manner in which passages are experienced by the person-in-transition.

Third, while recognizing the part played by social factors in precipitating role passage we have chosen to emphasize the *self-initiated* dimensions of a passage. In so doing, we call attention to persons as active role players who desire, and are capable of, shaping their social lives. As noted by Clausen (1968, p. 189), this is an important, although neglected, focus in much sociological research.

Fourth, the nature of our subject matter enabled us to examine the problems of *arrested passages* (Glaser & Strauss, 1971, p. 31) in which persons do not move with their peers through the typical sequence of roles associated with their age and sex. Arrested passages are examined in terms of their implications for the person's ability to negotiate role changes. These passages also are viewed as sources of change in the expected criteria for role incumbency.

Fifth, we have stressed the *processual* nature of role occupancy, viewing it as a dynamic process of continuous movement over a passage. To facilitate this perspective we have chosen to study the entire process of role passage including the three phases of role relinquishment, transition, and role acquisition rather than limiting it, as is more often done, to just one of these phases.

To the extent, of course, that other passages differ along these and related dimensions our insights and speculations have limitations. It is our belief, however, that by specifically focusing on these dimensions we have opened up areas of important concern that have yet to receive much attention in sociology.

We constructed our basic model of role passage by first asserting that the process involves at least three major sequences. Following Van Gennep's (1908) early statement of transitional phasing and a more recent conceptualization of the dynamic nature of status passage by Glaser and Strauss (1971), the process includes a *relinquishment* of one or more roles, a *transitional* phase of experimentation and learning, and the *acquisiton* of new roles. Our research, supported by other investigations of role passage (e.g., Becker, 1963; Goode, 1956; Humphreys, 1972; Rossi, 1968) leads us to affirm Becker's (1963) contention that explanatory variables are likely to be differentially significant at various stages in the overall passage.

Our findings lead to two further specifications regarding the phases of role passage. First, although it is analytically feasible to make rather clear distinctions among relinquishment, transition, and acquisition, in fact there is considerable overlapping between these sequences. Our discussions of the nun's inadvertent anticipatory socialization to secular roles, her deliberate role rehearsals for leaving, and her experience of passage lag in secular life all stress the overlap between and among these three general phases. Second, we found that within each major phase or sequence there exist subphases organized around special problems or dimensions of the passage (e.g., relinquishment of the religious role was a process that entailed motivation, preparation, and other phases). Each subphase involved different sets of variables to explain the outcomes at that point in the passage. Both these specifications serve to increase the complexity of the conceptual model and should sensitize the researcher to phenomena often obscured in more simplified views of passage sequences.

ROLE RELINQUISHMENT

Our initial conceptualization of relinquishment follows most closely the contributions by Brim and Wheeler (1966), Riley et al. (1969), Clausen (1968), and Riley et al. (1972) in that it stresses: (1) a view of relinquishment as involving processes that in large measure are the reverse of those entailed in the process of socialization, and (2) that, similar to socialization for role acquisition, relinquishment also depends on both individual and social contributions to the process.

Briefly we would say that for persons to *voluntarily* relinquish roles they must have the motivation to do so, they must be aware of existing structural alternatives, and they must define themselves as able to play alternative roles. These three requirements, in turn, depend on the social system providing clear norms for playing roles, opportunities to learn about and practice role expectations, and the distribution of sanctions for role performances. In addition, as Bredemeier and Stephenson (1962) observe, role relinquishment depends on the reduction of rewards for prior behavior. This reduction involves such processes as anticipatory socialization, changes in group memberships, shifts in reference groups and role models, and personal reassessments of meanings and events.

As a result of our findings, we can suggest the following additions to this part of the model. Regarding the individual variables of motivation, knowledge, and ability we found a *temporal* pattern to their appearance in the process of withdrawal from a role. Motivation to relinquish a role came first, followed by a search for alternative roles, and then an evaluation of one's ability to play alternative roles. It may be less important that this actual order occur in other instances or relinquishment than it is for us to be sensitive to the possibility that motives, knowledge, and perceived abilities may be differentially salient at various points in the process of relinquishment.

We also found a *reciprocal* relationship among these individual variables. Each of them feeds back into and affects the other two. For example, motivation or desire to reliquish a role may result in initiatives to seek out knowledge about role alternatives; or, increased confidence in one's abilities to play other roles may strengthen initial desires to relinquish a role. This, of course, implies that the relationship between individual and social contributions to relinquishment (as well as to role acquisition) have complex and often indirect interdependencies. We illustrate this point, for example, by showing that positive sanctions (a social contribution) for playing new roles not only directly reinforce motivation (an individual contribution) to leave a present role but also indirectly enhance perceived abilities (another individual contribution) to play new roles.

A model of role passage must include those analytical properties that differentiate among a variety of types of transitions—such as the extent to which a transition is desirable, reversible, or voluntary—because these properties will, to a significant extent, shape the interplay between individual and social variables already identified in the conceptual model. The most comprehensive attempt to both identify the major properties of passages and analyze their implications for the ways in which they are accomplished has been the formal theory offered by Glaser and Strauss (1971). In light of the type of passage studied here we included the following major properties as important in explaining the management of this particular passage: (1) the *voluntary* nature of the passage, (2) its *emergent* character, (3) the fact that it is a *solo* passage, and (4) the presence of a *multiple* passage. It was our contention that focusing on these four properties would serve to specify the relations between individual and social variables and to suggest ways in which certain theoretical problems take on special significance when viewed in the light of these properties.

The relinquishment of major roles, when analyzed in terms of these properties, leads to the following observations. First, the emergent nature of the transition places considerable responsibility on the individual for managing the intricacies and contingencies that surround the withdrawal from social roles. Unlike the situation in more institutionalized withdrawals, such as leaving educational and occupational roles, the absence of timetables, rules, customs, socializing agents, and facilitating resources places greater demands on the individual. She must, on her own or with the help of others, establish personal goals or aims, seek sources of information, devise measurements of one's abilties, negotiate an acceptable type of withdrawal, discover appropriate subsidiary agents—in sum, be both actor and agent in the process of relinquishment. The initiative, energy, intelligence, and endurance required of the individual underscore the often-neglected reliance by many persons on societal provisions to ease the institutionalized withdrawal from a variety of roles over the life course. In addition, the ease or difficulty of relinquishing roles and, to some extent, whether or not withdrawal eventually occurs, depends much more on variations in individual abilities, skills, and personality attributes in emergent as compared to conventional modes of relinquishment.

Second, even in solo forms of role-leaving the social environment can play a crucial part in facilitating relinquishment. For example, changes in the social system in which the role is embedded can generate desires for relinquishment; the media is an important organizer and distributor of information on alternative roles; peer groups may provide emotional support and distribute rewards; the leaving of roles by some may precipitate the conditions for the leaving by others; and role models and ideological groups can generate altered definitions of the situation. We have seen, in addition, that it is possible for role activities to serve as unintentional sources of anticipatory socialization and rehearsal for relinquishment, such as the changes in expectations for nuns as a result of Vatican Council II. These unintended consequences eased the women's subsequent accommodation to secular roles. For these reasons, an understanding of solo passage must be tempered by the observation that relinquishment always entails the participation of some others and is affected by social processes that surround the roles being relinquished.

Third, even though persons are engaged in a process of relinquishment of roles for which there is virtually no prior socialization, formal transitional agent, or precedent to guide withdrawal, they nevertheless make intentional preparations for leaving which they hope will facilitate subsequent adjustments to new roles. These preparations are guided by observations of past experiences in making other transitions, by commonsense assessments of the present situation, and by guidelines suggested by others who have recently given up the role and who thus can be viewed not only as agents in their own transition but also as subsidiary agents in the emerging transition of others. It is important to note that in this type of relinquishment preparations must be made in areas often not required in more institutionalized modes of role-leaving, such as the construction of explanations for relinquishment, the development of temporal strategies to avoid premature or delayed exits, and the selection among alternate modes of leaving. In light of our findings, we would support the hypothesis initially offered by Cottrell (1942) and Bredemeier and Stephenson (1962) that anticipatory socialization and role rehearsal eases subsequent acquisition of and accommodation to new roles. However, we would suggest that by virtue of the open-ended, underplanned character of emergent transitions the importance of anticipatory socialization and preparation is likely to be less than it is in more highly structured passages.

TRANSITION

Our conceptualization of the next phase as consisting of transitional steps that intervene between relinquishment and acquisition is derived from Glaser and Strauss (1971, p. 47) and strongly supported by the data. It is in these intermediate sequences that persons begin to forge new or modified relations with others, establish short-term ends and plan tactics to reach them, experiment and improvise with various types of behavior, and test and evaluate new presentations of self.

While transitional stages are institutionally predefined in more conventional passages, in emergent ones they are created or later reconstructed by the persons who are themselves going through the transition. Thus, one finds more variety in the number, duration, and type of transitional sequences in emergent passages which reflects the heterogeneity of individual skills, meanings, values, knowledge, and motives. However, certain uniformities in the phase did appear. First, the transitional phase was described as lasting approximately one year, suggesting that there may be some more general temporal boundary within which certain events occur that overrides variations between individuals. Second, the stage immediately following relinquishment is more expressive in nature than the subsequent ones which tend to have instrumental tasks as their primary focus. We interpret this pattern as reflecting the emotional unsettledness that accompanies role changes and which requires initial attention before persons can orient themselves to more instrumental activities.

Third, the persons-in-transit primarily act as their own agents in creating learning situations, seeking out sources of information, generating criteria for self-assessments, and planning temporal and substantive strategies for acquiring new roles and life-styles. The self-as-agent appears to be a double-edged situation in which, on the one hand, confusion, anxiety, and uncertainty are frequent components of emergent transitions (see Humphreys, 1972; Koffend, 1972; Skolnik, 1972); yet, on the other hand, it is precisely the absence of institutionalized formulations which have the benefit of allowing persons the freedom to regulate their passage in a manner that is responsive to individual needs, abilities, and wishes.

Fourth, this phase is characterized by frequent reassessments. Mistakes, miscalculations, premature moves, and tactical errors are "discovered" and attempts are made to rectify the situation, which then may result in new reference points, choices, and strategies. It is our impression that the emergent transition demands of persons a greater degree of self-reflection and self-evaluation than that required in more conventional transitions in which societal guidelines exist to socialize and allocate persons into and out of social roles.

Another characteristic theme is the underplanned nature of this phase due to the fact that this is a new transition lacking the scheduled character of well-known passages. The plans that are made can best be described as "mini-schedules" (Glaser & Strauss, 1971, p. 44) that serve to organize whatever tasks or short-term aims emerge or are created as the person moves along through the transition.

Even in solo transitions, persons will seek out and make use of subsidiary agents not only for role-learning but also to engage others in reciprocal relations and to elicit appropriate rewards for role performance and validations of successful role acquisition. This point has been most recently emphasized by Riley et al. (1972, p. 559) and, as we shall see later, serves to raise other questions about the modes of validation in emergent role transitions. We would like to stress two points here concerning the use of agents in emergent passages.

First, in such transitions the actors must seek out for themselves, and be able to judge the efficacy of, various potential subsidiary agents. Again this places the person-in-transit at a considersably greater risk than persons for whom agents are provided in more well-known passages. There is probably a greater likelihood in emergent transitions that the uninformed choices or judgments of appropriate agents will delay passage to certain roles, cause unwanted relational problems, or result in disarticulation between roles.

Second, as Bredemeier and Stephenson (1962, pp. 111–113) have suggested in their model of the socialization process, discrepancies in the expectations and abilities of socializing agents will hinder the ease with which new roles are learned and acquired. Our data not only support this observation but also point to a temporal dimension as well. We have incorporated Alice Rossi's (1968, p. 29) concept of the role cycle into our model to suggest that if we view a role as having a cycle in which each stage of the cycle has its unique tasks and adjustment problems then our findings point out that at each stage the appropriate socialization agents may also be different others. The task for individuals in an emergent transition is to become sensitive to the proper time at which to seek new agents or drop old ones. In addition, when persons are managing multiple transitions the complexity of this task increases because the stages of the various cycles of roles one is acquiring are not going to be at the same level of development. This makes the task of agent selection and evaluation a more complex and more difficult one. These observations also suggest that in studying emergent transitions the questions of timing, direction, and control of role transitions become important theoretical as well as substantive issues.

Our model proposes a view of role transition as a dynamic process in which persons move into and out of social roles over a particular time span. More specifically, we wish to emphasize that these movements do not occur in an unilinear, mechanical progression over fixed stages but rather consist of considerable overlapping between phases as actors shift back and forth between past and present roles. Our data, as well as supportive evidence from the general literature on socialization, have led us to propose an additional element in our conceptual framework to identify the appearance in the new passage of specific values, self-images, and habits of thought and behavior that are derived and carried over from the prior passage. We have termed this phenomenon "passage lag" and have identified at least two issues raised by the concept.

First, how does passage lag affect the accommodation to present roles and to the personal vicissitudes occasioned by role change? We have suggested that passage lag may function to smooth the transition to new roles insofar as person-in-transit can fall back on accustomed modes of definition and response to fill the structural vacuum that exists until they are more comfortable in their new roles. However, to the extent that successful role acquisition requires the *giving up* of past role behaviors, values, and definitions the persistence of these elements can clearly impede such acquisitions and delay the transformation of social identity.

Second, can the relative presence or absence of such traces from past roles signal the degree of adjustment persons are making to the overall transition? Our data show quite clearly that the dropping of traces from past roles accompanies shifts in reference groups, the learning and practice of new role expectations, and the receiving of rewards from others for successful role performance.

Virtually every model of role transition, including our initial conceptualization, focuses on the persons who are themselves engaged in role transfers and others who serve as transitional agents. The data from our study underscore the limitation of such a focus. When persons leave certain roles to move into other ones this activity always generates problems of accommodation and role-activation for others who have relational ties to the person-in-transit. It is our belief that this is a relatively neglected area of sociological inquiry. It can be a fruitful issue because it raises questions concerning the dynamics of reciprocal transitions and the mechanisms of mutual accommodation. It also provides an opportunity to extend our analysis beyond the micro level of the individual in a role to consider the dyadic nature of role passages (Riley, 1963, pp. 724–728). We would thus encourage a view of role transitions as *precipitating events* that may in effect launch others on a passage of their own to different roles, to modified arrangements within existing role relations, and to the activation of latent roles and identities.

By virtue of the fact that the transition under investigation involved a movement out of a total institution (Goffman, 1961) we had an opportunity to examine a phenomenon that is identified in the Glaser and Strauss model but not elaborated. According to these authors (Glaser & Strauss, 1971) leaving one passage "can turn out to yield an arrested passage" (p. 31). We found this property of arrestability to be useful in understanding the dynamics of the transition being studied and would encourage its incorporation into analyses of other transitions—such as the movement of women back into the labor force, the return of adults to higher education, the reentry of "deviants" into the community—as one way of theoretically tying together what are usually treated as more discrete phenomena. We can add to our model, then, the idea that, to varying degrees, the transition into certain roles may result in the postponement of passages to other roles thus causing them to become arrested.

Partial or total relinquishment of certain roles can then generate for individuals the problem of coming to terms with one or more of these arrested passages. The assumptions we are making here are that first, role-playing, like other skills, requires sufficient practice and polishing to maintain effectiveness (see Mann & Mann, 1959); second, that the normative content of roles may change over time and these alterations are less likely to be understood by persons not playing these roles with any frequency. Thus, when transitions turn out to yield arrested passages, persons-in-transit must determine what the modified configurations of expectations are in these roles and, in solo passages, must find ways to seek out appropriate sources of such information. In addition, if persons-in-transit wish to keep prior passages secret (e.g., ex-convict, ex-nun) then the processes of learning new expectations and seeking out socializing agents must be carried out in a circumspect manner for otherwise they may jeopardize the chances of successful passing (Goffman, 1963, p. 2).

In exploring the property of arrestability, we made use of the conceptualization offered by Riley et al. (1972, pp. 413–414) in which age is viewed as "a generalized status." Our data strongly support the view that an age category has attached to it an array of expectations predictive of behavior, knowledge, ability, sentiment, and the like. In addition to age as a generalized role, we know that there also exist certain age criteria for role occupancy or for engaging in particular types of behavior. Thus, one way in which passages become arrested occurs when persons fail to either relinquish or acquire roles in accordance with these generalized age expectations—for example, first marriage or initial job at the age of thirty-five. Riley et al. (1972) have provided us with an important concept, "age incongruity," to refer to violations "of age-related expectations or of age criteria for role incumbency" (p. 413). One of the sources of both personal anxiety and interactional strain in managing arrested passages can be viewed, then, as a result of age incongruity.

ACQUISITION

If we return, now, to our earlier contention that persons most frequently are involved in multiple role passages we can discuss the dual issue of priority and articulation identified by Glaser and Strauss (1971, p. 142) as being of central theoretical importance in understanding the negotiation of successful passages. In terms of managing priorities and modes of articulation, the ideal situation would be, for example, one in which agreed upon values govern the ranking of role requirements, and are supported by consistency in sanctions; the demands of different roles complemented and supported one another; societal mechanisms articulated multiple roles; the dictates of articulation were within the range of individual ability; the signs of poor articulation were clear and immediately evident; and the environment was benign or fortuitous. That this ideal situation seldom obtains has been widely noted by sociologists and has given rise to two well-known analyses of mechanisms of role articulation and modes of accommodation to role strain (Goode, 1960; Merton, 1968, pp. 425–433). In emergent passages the problems of priority and articulation are greater than in institutionalized ones where persons can rely, to a much larger extent, on the existence of norms, cultural preferences, schedules, ceremonies, and established priorities to facilitate articulation. The persons engaged in emergent passages must rely more fully on their own abilities to develop strategies, forge links, and make choices that will reduce the strains of disarticulated roles.

In examining the ways in which our respondents developed priority rankings for various roles we suggested that practical expediency plays a large part in shaping initial priorities, while role contingency (the extent to which successful movement into subsequent roles is contingent upon adequately managing prior ones) and the degree of control over role activities shapes later priority rankings. Periodic assessments lead to a continual reordering of priorities over time as persons shift tactics, juggle time, postpone events, and reallocate resources.

In analyzing the way in which persons respond to disarticulation we were led to make explicit what we believe are often neglected considerations behind discussions of strategies of articulation. Persons will vary in their ability to perceive, or to perceive early, the signs or poorly articulated roles. In addition to the fact that signs may be ambiguous or subtle in themselves, persons may also be differentially sensitive to making such "readings" and proceed to define strain in terms of personal inadequacy, bad luck, or some source other than social or structural ones. Also, we must be alive to the possibility that although persons may correctly identify structural strain they may vary in their perceived ability to ameliorate the situation. To neglect the part played by these factors in establishing articulation results in an overly mechanical view of the process of role articulation. It also results in a failure to explore the way in which, for example, socialization or ideology shapes the distribution of these variables among different segments of the population.

Finally, any model of role passage must include a set of ideas for explaining the way we understand and measure the extent to which persons succeed at role acquisitions. Before we can move to a consideration of this issue we must make another addition to the model—the link between social position and self-image. It is a fundamental sociological axiom that roles play a considerable part in shaping a person's self-image and identity. We would expect, then, that as persons move through various transitions their self-understandings and the imagery with which they define themselves will also undergo certain alterations. Indeed, a number of theoretical essays (Clausen, 1972; Erikson, 1950; Strauss, 1962) have explored the way in which the movement of persons over the life course, through varying complexes of roles and group memberships, generates conditions for the transformation of self. Our data are highly supportive of this view, showing clearly that as persons change their relations with others, take on new roles, alter their group affiliations, receive positive rewards for role performances, and become involved in new experiences, the ways in which they define and present themselves to others are revised or altered in the process.

If we understand role acquisitions as occasions for self-transformations then we can ask whether or not this conceptualization contains a suggestion for handling the issue of passage adjustment. Our position is that all role passages, to varying degrees, entail both personal and interactional problems to which some kind of adjustment must be made. Recognizing the ambiguous, value-laden qualities that adhere to the concept of "adjustment" we chose to employ conceptualization of this term that was proposed by Goode (1956, p. 19) in his study of the postdivorce adjustment process. Put briefly, we can say that the process of adjustment to role passage entails the incorporation of past roles, experiences, meanings, and self-images into the person's present life experiences in such a way that the individual's self-definition, behavior, and social identification are primarily grounded in present or future demands "rather than by constant reference to the ties defined by" prior roles (Goode, 1956, p. 241). Persons, then, can be viewed as having made an adjustment to a role passage to the extent that they come to define themselves in terms of roles and experiences grounded in their present life situation. Changes in self-imagery can thus serve as indicators or successful accommodation to role passage.

Implied in Goode's conceptualization and made more explicit in the model offered by Riley et al. (1972, p. 559) is the assertion that role acquisition requires the participation of some other to accept and validate claims to role occupancy. Persons are able to see themselves in roles only if others accord them that existence by making the appropriate reciprocal responses of related roles. We have, in effect, suggested the existence of both a psychological (self-image) and a sociological (allocation by others) measure of transitional adjustment. We also stressed their interdependence insofar as validating responses from others encourages new conceptions of self. These new self-images, in turn, increase the likelihood that role-appropriate behavior will follow and elicit further validation of one's self-image.

It is hoped that this elaboration of selected dimensions of emergent role passage will invite further modification and empirical examination in studies of other such passages.

13

Some Implications of Emergent Role Passage for Society

Even a cursory examination of American society yields an impression that it is characterized by continuous change in the role relations of its members and the institutions in which they participate. In just the past ten years we have witnessed significant changes in the university, the church, the business corporation, the family, and the military. We have seen shifts in the power relations between racial and ethnic groups, between the young and the aged, between the sexes, between city and suburb, and between producers and consumers. The paraprofessional, the single parent, the transsexual, and the systems analyst can be thought of as persons who are playing recently created roles that carry with them both new social identities and self-images. The existence of marriage by contract, continuing education, workshops on dying, and divorce kits are evidence that more traditional pathways into and out of adult roles are presently being revised. How can we account for these emergent passages and what are some of their implications for the larger society in which they are embedded?

One way of understanding these social experiments is to view them as consequences of processes that reflect changes in how a society is organized or functions. We might point to technological innovations, changes in birth rates and population patterns, ideological shifts, and scientific advances as examples of phenomena that generate the need, the opportunity, or the desire for persons to forge new roles or revise former ways of moving into and out of them. Of course, specific types of emergent passages are more closely tied to some rather than other social processes. For instance, the creation of new occupational roles is related to technological change; the changes in the roles played by minorities is grounded in legal, political, and ideological transformations; the shifts in transitions to adolescent and student roles are tied to labor market trends and other processes that shape the youth culture. As these and other examples reveal, we must be alive to how broad societal events trickle down the social structure and make themselves felt at the individual and group level.

Additional reflection indicates that the relation between societal changes and emergent passages is not just unidirectional. Emergent passages themselves may be sources of social change. The emergence of Blacks, hippies, gay activists, consumer advocacy, and draft resistance produced results which had far-reaching effects on the political and military institutions, the law and mass media, the family, and the school. Studies of the impact of campus radicalism on the organization of the university (Weaver & Weaver, 1969) or the influence of the feminist movement on legal and economic processes (Bernard, 1971) are but two substantive examples of how persons, through their construction of emergent passages, may not only be responding to societal change but also serving as active agents in such change. This realization calls attention to the interdependence between the individual and the society and to the dynamic reciprocity that is at the core of social life.

A second source of the emergent passage, perhaps a most profound one, is a change in consciousness by members of society about their participation in social life. A diverse group of social thinkers—C. Wright Mills (1959), Paulo Freire (1968), Herbert Marcuse (1964), Peter Berger (1963), Charles Reich (1970)—have suggested that we are now on the threshold of a radical change in consciousness which, more than mere technological or scientific advance, will serve to dramatically alter modern society. Halpern (1969) most effectively characterizes this capacity for social transformation:

> Modern consciousness in relation to society and history is constituted of an awareness that there are patterns in the encounter of individuals, groups and concepts, that these patterns have been developed by man, these patterns are breaking, and that they can be transformed by man. (p. 69)

It is our belief that the larger number of persons in our society are acting in "bad faith" (Berger, 1963, pp. 143–145)—making the expectations of their roles serve as a flight from personal choice and responsibility. However, there is a growing number of people who recognize that reality is a social construction; that rules, roles, and institutions are capable of being altered; that alternatives to existing social structures can and should be created. We interpret the emergent passages of minorities, youth, women, the aged, homosexuals, soldiers, and nuns as reflecting this changing consciousness. We do not mean to imply that in a very short time most people will begin to critically evaluate present roles and traditional pathways through them, striking out on their own or with others to create new ones. Nor do we infer that these emergent passages will be met with only positive rewards and congratulations by others. Sociological wisdom itself has stressed the protective, supportive functions of taken-for-granted structures that would militate against the first possibility; we have sufficient documentation of the frequency with which violations of social expectations are punished to also make the second possibility rather unlikely. Nevertheless, this new consciousness, which is sociological in nature and envisions social roles and institutions as amenable to change, is slowly but certainly spreading through the social order. Even in the more traditional pockets of social life—among white ethnics, police officers, professional athletes—we have begun to see a new awareness that demands greater participation in shaping the meanings and goals of the roles people play.

Indeed, it is somewhat ironic that over the last decade we witnessed an incongruous shift in those groups who espouse this new consciousness and protest their social impotence. In the late sixties police officers battled emerging war resisters, athletes ridiculed the cries of exploitation by campus radicals, white ethnics opposed Black power, and consumers ignored the grape boycotts. Today, police officers strike for greater autonomy, athletes organize themselves as an exploited class, white ethnics feel powerless and protest "reverse discrimination," and consumers boycott sugar and coffee. This phenomenon suggests to us that emergent passages in themselves give rise to others. This "contagion effect" would then be a third source of the increase in emergent passages in our society. This of course happened in the sixties among "out groups"—those who in fact had little power in defining their personal and social identities. On the heels of the Black Power consciousness and its demands for institutional change came the New Left, campus radicalism, the hippie movement, feminism, and gay activism. Each group provided examples of how to raise questions and identify problems about control over their life space. It was not long before other outsiders—the aged, the dying, prisoners, the handicapped—followed suit. Today, we see this emerging consciousness developing among some "insiders" as well, as they improvise new ways to live, or new pathways to get where they are going.

What might these events mean for our society? Of all the possible implications that we invite the reader to pursue, we will examine just four general ones. The first implication may be termed *social transcience*. Although many people may break out of conventional roles and pathways in order to mold new kinds of social lives, certainly not all, nor even most, will be successful in completing their passage. If this is a possibility even in highly scheduled passages, then it would be even more likely to happen in emergent ones. Our own findings on former nuns, reports of some women who have left the traditional female role (Breslin, 1973), observations on ex-Communists (Wright, 1949), and recent reports of the present situation of hippies, street people, campus radicals, and Vietnam veterans highlight the very real possibility of persons becoming stranded along the way toward new identities and social places. In some sense they can be seen as marginal persons suspended between the past roles they relinquish and the newly formulated ones that others have been more successful at creating. What alternatives may exist for these persons? We can think of at least four possibilities. Some may take refuge at the edges of the communities of their former commitment and affiliation; for example, former nuns who remain active in religious groups, former Communists who drift near the boundaries of local radical pockets, or former hippies who keep in contact with communal life. Another possibility is to drift from one emerging group to another, such as New Left women who transferred to Women's Liberation, or campus radicals who had come from Black power groups, or hippies who later "turned on" to the Jesus movement. Given the frequency with which emerging groups arise on the social scene, it would not be difficult for some persons to launch themselves into a seemingly endless series of such affiliations. Still others may succumb to the emotional strain of marginality and suffer psychological and physical trauma. Finally, there exists the possibility of returning to one's prior roles and life-style, although it would require some degree of personal conversion to make one's way back home again.

In turn, as increasing numbers of persons move out of institutionalized pathways—unprotected by schedules, rules, customs, definitions, and ceremonies—we may see an increase in the number of such people adrift in society. Their need for support, guidance, affiliation, and recognition will heighten the demand for transitional agencies to help ease them through these passages. Our data, as well as findings from other investigations of emergent passages (Breslin, 1973; Humphreys, 1972; Kubler-Ross, 1969; Wright, 1949), indicate that all emergent passages are frequently accompanied by stress, confusion, ambivalence, and insecurity. This means that the society will be called upon to provide different types of transitional agencies than those already available for traditional passages. In some instances, persons who have already made substantial strides in their own emergent passages have spontaneously established informal transitional agencies to ease the passage of others. For example, women's consciousness-raising cells, "free" universities, singles communities, gay counseling centers, and widowhood groups are serving this need. In other instances transitional agencies are provided by outsiders, experts, or more formal socializing agents such as is the case in Black Studies Centers, open-admissions programs, drug clinics, retirement communities, and seminars on dying. We would expect to see in the near future an increase in these transitional agencies. In fact, in discussing social strategies for coping with future shock, Toffler (1970, pp. 371–397) calls for such agencies to ease the adjustment to rapid technological change.

A second implication of the proliferation of emergent passages concerns the issue of *social control* in a society. Every society formally assigns official authority to particular agents for socializing and allocating persons to roles. These institutionalized agents of social control—parents, teachers, employers, doctors—may find their power and control over transitions decreasing as they lose their monopoly over important resources and rewards. For example, the power of professors over students is weakened to the degree that students cannot find employment, do not value the conventional rewards of occupational careers, or select other pathways to economic survival. The medical and psychiatric professions have had to yield some of their sphere of influence to self-help practitioners, sexual therapists, and gurus who have sprung up around the emergent passages of others. Clergymen have found that major inroads in their locus of control have been made by shamans, exorcists, lay priests, and self-proclaimed prophets. Lawyers now confront citizens who want to serve as their own attorneys and men find women building their own bookstores, banks, and restaurants. As persons begin to function as their own agents; as they reject traditional values and norms to proclaim different ones; as they demand more autonomy over their lives; as they are able to find new sources of information, support, learning, and validation they will weaken the traditional alliances between themselves and agencies of social control. Although there are, and will surely continue to be, struggles to gain or retain control over role passages, we cannot help but believe that the sheer amount of control previously exercised by men, whites, adults, schools, doctors, and employers, for example, has been systematically eroded in many areas of society.

A third implication of emergent passages has to do with *organizational planning and effectiveness*. In these passages, unlike more highly scheduled ones, temporal expectations are vague or unknown. Decisions concerning the "right time" to make certain moves become more individualized. This, we expect, will be of increasingly greater concern for people in advanced societies as conventional temporal guidelines prove less desirable and less effective for meeting personal and social needs. When to marry? When to begin work? When to go to college? When to retire? When to die? As timings for role relinquishment and acquisition become more heterogeneous and person-alized, this will create problems of accommodations in organizations and agencies because these associations depend, in large part, on the aggregate movement of significant numbers of persons in and out of roles at approximately similar ages and temporal intervals. In high schools, for example, there are already structural changes that make it possible for young adults to engage in part-time employment and part-time schooling. Universities are instituting "continuing education" programs and "week-end colleges" that respond to the needs of the nontraditional student. Business firms are experimenting with intermittent career trajectories and partial-retirement policies. These and similar changes in organizations are the result, to some extent, of emergent passages. The fact is that the calculations by organizations for markets, services, budgets, and resources are based on temporal estimates of role transfers and the manner in which these transfers will occur. Therefore, changes in these temporal estimates and traditional pathways will exert pressure on organizations to make appropriate modifications. Unfortunately, most organizations are not arranged to be sufficiently flexible to meet these changing demands. This lag between what organizations offer and what people want is another constant source of tension between the individual and the society. In a more positive vein, resolutions of these tensions will make organizations more pluralistic as they adapt to the differing rhythms of subgroups in the society.

The fourth and final implication of emergent passages focuses on the process of *socialization* by which individuals come to acquire the necessary skills, knowledge, and values needed to perform adequately in their roles. Emergent transitions—passages into the social unknown—require specific abilities, personality traits, values, and orientations that call for changes in the way in which persons are usually socialized for adult roles. Specifically, these passages require self-reliance and a willingness to take control over the shape and direction of one's life. One needs an ability to tolerate ambiguity, to make critical assessment and to establish guidelines for planning and pacing one's life course. One has to develop skills for risk-taking and decision-making. Most importantly one must value personal change, diversity, and social flux.

Gail Sheehy (1976), in *Passages,* effectively captures the personality changes common to each stage of adult life. She identifies, on the psychological level, the critical turning points of adult development and the demands and challenges they make on the adult personality. Social theorists have delineated the types of changes in social structure that can be expected in the very near future (Bennis, 1970; Silberman, 1970; Toffler, 1972). It almost seems necessary to put in quotation marks some of the following projected roles and behavior—professional parents, psychosurgeons, thematic colleges, cloned children, biofeedback medicine, acquacommunities, and the like. To increase the individual's ability to adapt to such continual change, and to successfully negotiate passages into emerging social locations, it may also be necessary to emphasize *partial* rather than *total* commitment to social roles. In fact, one of the sources of considerable strain in all passages is due precisely to the difficulty of motivating persons who have made strong commitments to present roles, and who find them comfortable, to then relinquish them. Socialization that encourages maximum commitment to major adult roles may make it more difficult for persons to adapt to divorce, the leave-taking of children from the family, career changes, retirement, and widowhood, to name but a few. It also makes more difficult the ability to adjust to changes in the social environment that require or make attractive such passages. One could even argue that this type of socialization is rapidly becoming anachronistic in a society characterized by much personal and societal change. The more strongly committed we are to present roles and relations, the greater investment we have in them, the more difficult it will be to relinquish them and be receptive to new arrangements. The dilemma, of course, is that without rigorous training for and commitment to roles people may not follow social expectations as closely and social order will be harder to maintain. In this vein, Riley et al. (1972) cogently observe that while limited commitment to roles can facilitate relinquishment it "also enlarges the potential for deviant role behavior. And, ultimately, limited commitment, as it reduces role expectations, can completely change the goals and norms of the role itself" (p. 538). It is this last point which we believe best describes the thrust of many present emergent passages. The willingness of persons to strike out on their own, to reshape customary pathways and conventional roles, to relinquish social locations that they no longer find rewarding, and to make commitments that are open to revision is responsible for not a small amount of contemporary social change and individual promise.

Appendix:
Interview Guide

The interview guide used in this study consisted of both standardized and nonstandardized interview questions (Richardson, Dohrenwend, & Klein, 1965, pp. 32–55). All the standardized questions have been included in the interview guide as well as the major nonstandardized ones. In discussing more complex and delicate topics with respondents, I relied on a range of nonstandardized probe questions. The major issues and areas that were probed are included in parentheses. The interview guide has been organized in a logical sequence that is aimed at aiding the reader. In the actual course of the interviews, however, the sequence of questions and probes were ordered to meet the demands of the interview process.

A. BACKGROUND INFORMATION
ON RESPONDENTS

Educational level at time of entrance into religious life.
Date of entrance into religious life.
Age at entrance into religious life.
Number of years spent in religious life.
Type of vow taken at time of leave of absence/dispensation.
Educational level at time of leave of absence/dispensation.
Date of withdrawal (leave/dispensation) from religious life.
Age at time of withdrawal from religious life.
Present occupation.
Present marital status.
Present place of residence.

Occupation of father/mother.

Number of children in family.

Type of high school attended (public, private/Catholic, private/non-Catholic).

B. THE PROCESS OF RELINQUISHMENT

What was it like to be a nun when you first entered religious life? (Probe for expectations, degree of satisfaction with religious and community role; impact of convent socialization.)

When did you first begin to question religious life and your role as a nun? (Probe for respondent's involvements and relations at this time: her activities in the convent, group memberships, friends, secular activities.)

How did you feel about the suggested changes for religious communities stemming from Vatican Council II?

How involved were you in your community's response to these changes? How did you feel about these changes?

Under what circumstances did you first think about the possibility of leaving religious life? (Probe for the possible sources of this idea, respondent's reaction to this possibility, and her feelings about leaving.)

With whom, if anyone, did you discuss the idea of leaving? (Probe for talks with peers, Superiors, priest–confessor, family; try to ascertain the impact of such exchanges on respondent's own thoughts and feelings about leaving.)

How did you feel about the fact that other nuns were leaving your community? (Probe for impact of other's leaving on respondent's decision to stay or leave.)

What were your own thoughts and feelings about the possibility of your leaving? (Probe for awareness of alternatives to religious life and estimates of ability to make it in the secular society.)

Were there any significant events or factors that influenced your decision to leave? (Probe for both changes within the community and events external to the community.)

Why do you think you decided to leave the convent? (Probe for respondent's attitudes toward changes in the structure of religious life and the fit between personality and the role of nun.)

Did your behavior as a nun change at all before you left? In what way? (Probe for deviations from the norms of religious life.)

How difficult was it for you to come to the decision to leave? (Probe for possible resistance to leaving; physiological or emotional disturbances.)

Before you left, did you make any plans for what you would do when you got out? (Probe for choice of residence, job, preparing family, shopping, and so on.)

How did you feel about the changes in the habit? What was it like to go into the modified habit? (Probe for effects on self-image, salience of sex role, responses from others, reactions to others.)

Did you ask for a leave of absence or a dispensation? Why?

What did you think it would be like when you left? (Probe for expectations, goals, estimates of the difficulty or ease of the transition.)

C. TRANSITIONAL PHASES

Can you describe what it was like the day you left? How did you feel? What was your reaction to being out of the convent?

Tell me about your first few weeks out of the convent. What did you do? How did you feel? Where did you go? (Probe here for any new experiences, accommodations, and activities and respondent's responses to them.)

Where did you live after you first left the convent? (Probe for reasons for choice of residence and adjustment to nonconvent living arrangements.)

(If respondent went home) What was it like to be home again with your family? (Probe for resumption of kin roles and respondent's accommodation to being home.)

(If respondent did not go home) Were your relations with your family any different once you left? In what ways? Did your family assist you in any way in making the transition? Did your family relations hinder your transition in any way?

Was there anything new you experienced once you came out? Was there anything you had to learn or adjust to that was not familiar to you? (Probe for personal and social facts: shopping for clothes, makeup, budgeting, banking, parties, meeting new people and so forth.)

How did people who knew you as a nun react to you once you left the convent? Was there any change in their relation to you? How did you feel about this? (Probe for salience of religious role, ambivalent responses, stereotyping.)

How often did you think about the convent when you first came out? How frequently did you visit the convent, if at all? How much did you talk about the convent? (Probe for any changes in these areas over time.)

Did you go to a transitional agency for exreligious at any time? Why?

D. ROLE ACQUISITIONS

Work

What occupation did you first have after leaving religious life? (Probe for how respondent obtained position and reasons for seeking this occupation.)

In what ways, if any, was your work different from that in religious life? (Probe for orientations toward employment, colleague relationships, adjustment to secular work roles.)

Did your co-workers know you had been a nun? (Probe for respondent's desire and ability to control this information and her reactions to possible disclosure.)

Have you had any other employment since this first position? (Probe for reasons.)

How satisfied are you with your present occupation? Why?

How confident do you feel in the working world? (Probe for occupational adjustments, development of friendships with co-workers, changes in attitudes toward work since leaving the convent.)

Age

When you first came out, did you feel that you fit in socially with other women your age? (Probe for arrested age passage in areas of work, dating and marriage, friendship and social activities, level of maturation.)

Do you think that during the time you have been out of religious life you have become more in tempo with women your own age? How would you explain this?

Do you feel that your age influenced, in any way, your work? friendships? dating partners? relations with family? (Probe for age incongruities; comparisons with former nuns younger or older than respondent.)

Are there any ways in which age affects the overall transition to secular life? Could you describe them?

Sex Role

When you were in the convent, how aware were you of being a woman? Has there been any change since you left? (Probe for salience of female role; sources of suppression and maintenance of female role in religious life; factors involved in any changes in awareness.)

How would you define the role of a woman from your own perspective? What do you think about the Women's Liberation Movement? (Probe for respondent's orientation to the role of woman and the possible influence of convent life on her conception of the role.)

Are your relations with women any different now than when you were in the convent? (Probe for differences in qualities of relations: cooperation, competition, and function of woman as reference points for female role.)

Romance and Sexuality

When you were in the convent were you ever romantically involved with anyone? (Probe for type of person: priest, lay-person; length of relation; extent of physical involvement; frequency of involvements.)

How did you feel about your involvement in this relationship? (Probe for attempt to conceal, confiding in others; effect of relationship on decision to leave, and on the salience of the female role.)

What was your dating life like before entering the convent? (Frequency, length, degree of involvement, and sexual experience.)

Have you dated since leaving the convent? (Source of dating partner: known or involved with in convent or new acquaintance; time of first date, circumstance; frequency of dating, sexual involvement.)

Could you describe your first date? (Probe for presence of dating skills, confidence in dating role, reactions to partner.)

How do you go about meeting dating partners? (Probe for use of friends, groups, singles clubs; degree of difficulty or ease in meeting partners.)

How confident do you feel in dating now? What factors account for this?

What are your feelings about sexual involvement before marriage? (Probe for present sexual experience; norms regarding sexual activity.)

(If respondent was on a leave) Did being under vows affect your dating and sexual involvements? In what ways? To what degree?

(If respondent is married) Tell me about your marriage. How did you meet your husband? How long did you date? How soon after leaving did you marry? How would you evaluate your marriage? (Probe for extent to which respondent defines marriage as index of successful transition: what effect did being a nun have on reactions of spouse and others to the marriage; plans for children.)

Friendship

Who were your closest friends when you first left the convent?

Who are closest friends now? (Probe for friends before entering, other ex-nuns, new associates.)

Has your circle of friends changed since you have left? (Probe for shifts in friendship circle.)

What are the advantages and disadvantages of having ex-nuns as friends? (Probe for support through transition, socialization, impact on other status acquisitions, impediments to transition.)

Religion

Have your religious beliefs changed at all since you left? Religious practices? In what way? (Probe for degree and type of change; impact of changes on status acquisitions; for example, on family relations, dating, and so forth.)

What is your attitude toward religious life and the role of nun?

Were there any advantages to having been in the convent? disadvantages?

E. SELF-IMAGE AND PERSONALITY

Do you feel that you are any different as a person now from when you were a nun? (Probe for a change in personality in convent, feelings of autonomy, maturation, self-interest.) What factors account for this change?

How would you describe yourself? What kind of a person are you? (Probe for perceived influence of personality attributes on transition.)

Have others perceived any changes in you? (Probe for evaluation of the change as positive or negative and effect on respondent's own image.)

Did you ever define yourself as an ex-nun? What did that mean to you? Do you still see yourself in that way? Why? (Probe for salience of role on present self-image.)

Has your view of the world changed since leaving? How? (Probe for differences in values, meanings, assessments of people, events.)

F. BIOGRAPHICAL INFORMATION AND PRESENTATION OF SELF

Do you have a policy about informing others that you were once a nun? (Probe for what information was given, to whom, at what point, and why; changes over time.)

What kinds of reactions did you get from others when they found out you had been in the convent? (Probe for differences in reactions by particular others: dating partners, employers, work peers; probe for stereotypical reactions.) How did you respond?

Once others knew you were an ex-nun, did you feel that they expected you to behave in certain ways? How?

Some people say that they can recognize women who were once nuns—that some women look like "ex-nuns"—how do you feel about this? (Probe for content of image as "ex-nun"; did respondent ever think she looked like an ex-nun and what tactics, if any, did she use to control her image?)

G. GENERAL DIMENSIONS OF ROLE PASSAGE

In looking over the time since you've been out, do you feel that you have made the transition to secular life? (Probe for degree of completion, criteria used, length of time it took or expected to take.)

What were the easiest and more difficult aspects of the transition?

Did you experience the transition to secular life as a series of steps or stages along the way? Are there any strategic or turning points that you recognize?

Was there any discrepancy between what you expected the transition would be like and how you experienced it?

Considering all the adjustments that must be made when people change their life-style, did you establish any priorities for dealing with them? (Probe for ranking of activities, motives for ranking, changes in priorities; probe for sources of competition and cooperation between various areas of role acquisition.)

References

Abbot, W. M., S.J. (Ed.), *The documents of Vatican II.* New York: America Press, 1966.

Appley, D. G. The changing place of work for women and men. In A. G. Sargent (Ed.), *Beyond sex roles.* New York: West Publishing Co., 1977. Pp. 300–318.

Aries, E. Male–female interpersonal styles in all male, all female and mixed groups. In A. G. Sargent (Ed.), *Beyond sex roles.* New York: West Publishing Co., 1977. Pp. 292–299.

Aronson, H. New girls back in town. *Cosmopolitan,* December 1971, 196–200.

Atwater, L. Managing violated expectancies: the age deviant in interaction. Unpublished paper presented at the Annual Meeting of the American Sociological Association, New York, New York, 1973.

Atwater, L. Women in extramarital relationships: a case study in sociosexuality. Ph.D. Dissertation, Rutgers University, 1978.

Baldwin, M. *I leap over the wall.* New York: Rinehart, 1950.

Banton, M. *Roles: An introduction to the study of social relations.* New York: Basic Books, 1965.

Bardwick, J. *Psychology of women.* New York: Harper & Row, 1971.

Becker, H. *Outsiders—Studies in the sociology of deviance.* New York: The Free Press, 1963.

Bennis, W. (Ed.) *American bureaucracy.* Chicago: Aldine, 1970.

Berger, P. *Invitation to sociology.* New York: Doubleday, 1963.

Bernard, J. *Women and the public interest.* Chicago: Aldine, 1971.

Booth, A. Sex and social participation. *American Sociological Review,* 1972, *37,* 183–193.

Bredemeier, H. C., & Stephenson, R. M. *The analysis of social systems.* New York: Holt, Rinehart, & Winston, 1962.

Breslin, C. Waking up from the dream of women's lib. *New York,* February 26, 1973, 30–38.

Brim, O., & Wheeler, S. *Socialization after childhood.* New York: Wiley, 1966.

Brownmiller, S. *Against our will: Men, women and rape.* New York: Simon & Schuster, 1975.

Bullough, V. L. *The subordinate sex.* Urbana, Ill: University of Illinois Press, 1973.

Chafetz, J. S. *Masculine/feminine or human?* Itasca, Illinois: Peacock, 1974.

Cita-Malard, S. *Religious orders of women.* New York: Hawthorne, 1964.

Clausen, J. (Ed.), *Socialization and society.* Boston: Little, Brown, 1968.

Clausen, J. The life course of individuals. In M. W. Riley, M. Johnson, & A. Foner (Eds.), *Aging and society,* Vol. 3. New York: Russell Sage, 1972. Pp. 457–514.

Cottrell, L. The adjustment of the individual to his age and sex roles *American Sociological Review, 1942, 7,* 617–620.

Daly, M. *The church and the second sex* (with a new feminist post-Christian introduction by the author). New York: Harper & Row, Colophon Books, 1975.

Deutscher, I. Socialization for postparental life. In A.M. Rose (Ed.), *Human behavior and social processes.* Boston: Houghton-Mifflin, 1962.

Doely, S. B. (Ed.) *Women's liberation in the church.* New York: Association Press, 1970.

Dunham, W. H. *Community and schizophrenia: An epidemiological analysis.* Detroit: Wayne State Univ. Press, 1965.

Ebaugh, H. R. F. *Out of the cloister: A study of organizational dilemmas.* Austin, Texas: Univ. of Texas Press, 1977.

Ellis, R., & Lane, W. C. Social mobility and social isolation: A test of Sorokin's dissociative hypothesis. *American Sociological Review, 1967, 32,* 237–253.

Erikson, E. *Childhood and society.* New York: Norton, 1950.

Erikson, E. *Identity, youth and crisis.* New York: Norton, 1968.

Farrell, W. *The liberated man: Beyond masculinity.* New York: Random House, 1974.

Freeman, J. (Ed.) *Women: A feminist perspective.* Palo Alto, California: Mayfield, 1975.

Freire, P. *Pedagogy of the oppressed* (orig. publ. 1968), (M. Bergman Ramos, trans.). New York: The Seabury Press, 1970.

Gagnon, J., & Simon, W. *Sexual conduct: The social sources of human sexuality.* Chicago: Aldine, 1973.

Garfinkle, H. Conditions of successful degradation ceremonies. *American Journal of Sociology,* 1956, *61,* 420-424.

Garfinkle, H. Common-sense knowledge of social structures - the documentary method of interpretation. In J. M. Scher (Ed.), *Theories of the minds.* New York: The Free Press of Glencoe, 1962. Pp. 689–712.

Garfinkle, H. *Studies in ethnomethodology.* Englewood Cliffs, N.J.: Prentice Hall, 1967.

Glaser, B., & Strauss, A. Awareness contexts and social interaction. *American Sociological Review,* 1964, *29,* 669–679.

Glaser, B., & Strauss, A. *Status passage.* Chicago: Aldine, 1971.

Gluckman, M. (Ed.) *Essays on the ritual of social relations.* Manchester, England: Manchester Univ. Press, 1962.

Goffman, E. *The presentation of self in everyday life.* Garden City, New York: Doubleday Anchor, 1959.

Goffman, E. *Asylums.* New York: Anchor Books, 1961.

Goffman, E. *Stigma: Notes on the management of spoiled identity.* Englewood Cliffs, N.J.: Prentice Hall, 1963.

Goode, W. J. *After divorce.* New York: Free Press, 1956.

Goode, W. J., A theory of role strain. *American Sociological Review,* 1960, *25,* 483-496.

Goslin, D. A. (Ed.) *Handbook of socialization theory and research.* Chicago: Rand McNally, 1969.

Gouldner, F. Demotion in industrial management. *American Sociological Review,* 1965, *30,* 714–724.

Griffin, M. *The courage to choose: An American nun's story.* Boston: Little, Brown, 1975.

Gross, E. *Work and society.* New York: Thomas Y. Crowell, 1958.

Hageman, A. L. (Ed.) *Sexist religion and women in the Church — No more silence.* New York: Association Press, 1974.

Halpern, M. A redefinition of the revolutionary situation. *Journal of International Affairs,* 1969, *23,* 54–75.

Harbeson, G. E. *Choice and challenge for the American woman.* Cambridge, Mass.: Schenkman, 1971.

Hiestand, D. *Changing careers after thirty-five.* New York: Columbia Univ. Press, 1971.

Hughes, E. C. Dilemmas and contradictions of status. *American Journal of Sociology*, 1945, *50*, 353–359.

Humphreys, L. *Out of the closets — The sociology of homosexual liberation*. Englewood Cliffs, N.J.: Prentice Hall, 1972.

Hyman, H. *Political socialization*. New York: The Free Press of Glencoe, 1959.

Janeway, E. *Man's world, woman's place: A study in social mythology*. New York: Delta, 1971.

Jehenson, R. B. The dynamics of role leaving: A role theoretical approach to the leaving of religious organizations. *Journal of Applied Behavioral Science*, 1969, *5*, 287–308.

Joseph, N., & Alex, N. The uniform: A sociological perspective. *American Journal of Sociology*, 1972, *77*, 4 (January) 719–730.

Kavanagh, J. *A modern priest looks at his outdated church*. New York: Trident Press, 1967.

Kelly, R. M., & Boutilier, M. A. *The making of political women*. Chicago: Nelson-Hall, 1978.

Kennedy, D. B., & Kerber, A. *Resocialization — An American experiment*. New York: Behavioral Publications, 1972.

Koffend, J. A letter to my wife on the breakup of our marriage. *New York Magazine*, April 10, 1972, 29–37.

Koltun, E. (Ed.) *The Jewish woman: New perspectives*. New York: Schocken, 1976.

Kubler-Ross, E. *On death and dying*. New York: Macmillan, 1969.

Laws, J. L., & Schwartz, P. *Sexual scripts: The social construction of female sexuality*. Hinsdale, Ill: The Dryden Press, 1977.

Lefton, M., Skipper, J. K. Jr., & McCaghy, C. H. (Eds.) *Approaches to deviance*. New York: Appleton-Century-Crofts, 1968.

Lindesmith, A. R. *The addict and the law*. Bloomington, Ind.: Indiana Univ. Press, 1965.

Maccoby, E. E., & Jacklin, C. N. *The psychology of sex differences*. Stanford, Cal.: Stanford Univ. Press, 1974.

Mann, J. H., & Mann, C. H. The effect of role-playing experience on role-playing ability. *Sociometry*, 1959, *22*, 64–74.

Marcuse, H., *One dimensional man*. Boston: Beacon Press, 1964.

Masters, W. H., & Johnson, V. E. *Human sexual response*. Boston: Little, Brown, 1966.

Merton, R. K. *Social theory and social structure*. New York: Free Press 1968.

Millum, T. *Images of women: Advertising in women's magazines*. London: Chatts & Windus, 1975.

Mills, C. W., *The sociological imagination*. New York: Oxford Univ. Press, 1959.

Molitor, Sister M. M. A. A comparative study of dropouts and nondropouts in a religious community. Ph.D. Dissertation, Catholic University of America, 1967.

Muckenhirn, Sister M. C. B., E. S. C. (Ed.) *The new nuns*. New York: New American Library,1967.

Neal, Sister M. A., S. N. D. Stirrings in the religious life. Unpublished paper presented to Vocation Conferences in Boston, New York, and Rochester, May–June, 1968.

Nisbet, R. A. *The social bond*. New York: Knopf, 1970.

Papa, M., Sisters embark on "pilgrim road." *National Catholic Reporter*, August 27, 1971, *7*, 38, 2.

Pittman, D. J. (Ed.) *Alcoholism*. New York: Harper & Row, 1967.

Pogrebin, L. C. Competing with women. *Ms. Magazine*, July 1972, 78–81, 131.

Reich, C. A. *The greening of America*. New York: Random House, 1970.

Reiss, I. *Premarital sexual standards in America*. New York: The Free Press, 1960.

Richardson, S., Dohrenwend, B.S., & Klein, D. *Interviewing—Its forms and functions*. New York: Basic Books, 1965.

Riley, M. W. *Sociological research-A case approach*. New York: Harcourt, Brace, & World, 1963.

Riley, M. W., Johnson, M., & Foner, A. Socialization for the middle and later years. In D. A.

Goslin (Ed.), *Handbook of socialization theory and research*. Chicago: Rand McNally, 1969.

Riley, M. W., Johnson, M., & Foner, A. *Aging and society*, Vol. 3. New York: Russell Sage, 1972.

Rosow, I. *Socialization to old age*. Berkeley: Univ. of California Press, 1975.

Rossi, A. Transition to parenthood. *Journal of Marriage and the Family*, February 1968, *30,* 26–39.

Rubington, E., & Weinberg, M. S. (Eds.) *Deviance—The interactionist perspective*. New York: MacMillan, 1968.

Ruether, R. *Religion and sexism: Images of women in the Jewish and Christian traditions*. New York: Simon & Schuster, 1974.

Safilios-Rothschild, C. *Women and social policy*. Englewood Cliffs, N.J.: Prentice Hall, 1974.

Safilios-Rothschild, C. *Love, sex, and sex roles*. Englewood Cliffs, N.J.: Prentice Hall, 1977.

Scheff, T.J. (Ed.) *Mental illness and social processes*. New York: Harper & Row, 1967.

Schur, E. M. *Crimes without victims: Deviant behavior and public policy*. Englewood Cliffs, N.J.: Prentice Hall, 1965.

Scott, M. B., & Lyman, S. M. Accounts. *American Sociological Review*, 1963, *33*, 46–62.

Sheehy, G. *Passages: Predictable crises of adult life*. New York: Dutton, 1976.

Sherif, C. W. Females in the competitive process. In G .H. Sage (Ed.), *Sport and American society*, 2nd ed. Reading, Mass.: Addison-Wesley, 1974. Pp.314–340.

Silberman, C. E. *Crisis in the classroom*. New York: Random House, 1970.

Simmons, J. L. *Deviants*. Berkeley: Glendessary, 1969.

Skolnik, J. Notes of a recycled housewife. *New York Magazine,* May 22, 1972, 36–40.

Smigel, E. O. *The Wall Street lawyer*. New York: Free Press, 1965.

Stone, G. Appearance and the self. In A. Rose (Ed.), *Human behavior and social processes*. Boston: Houghton Mifflin, 1962. Pp. 86–118.

Strauss, A. *Mirrors and masks*. Illinois: The Free Press, 1959.

Strauss, A. Transformation of identity. In A. Rose (Ed.), *Human behavior and social processes*. Boston: Houghton Mifflin, 1962. Pp. 63–85.

Suenens, Cardinal L. J. *The nun in the world*. Maryland: Newman Press, 1962.

Tiger, L. *Men in groups*. New York: Random House, 1969.

Toffler, A. *Future shock*. New York: Random House, 1970.

Toffler, A. (Ed.) *The futuristists*. New York: Random House, 1972.

Turner, R. H. Role-taking, role standpoint, and reference-group behavior. *American Journal of Sociology*, 1956, *61*, 316-328.

Van Gennep, A. *The rites of passage*. (orig. publ. 1908) (M. B. Vizedom & G. L. Caffee, trans.). Chicago: Univ. of Chicago Press, Phoenix Books, 1960.

Weaver, G. R., & Weaver, J. H. (Eds.) *The university and revolution*. Englewood Cliffs, N.J.: Prentice Hall, 1969.

Westhues, K. *The religious community and the secular state*. New York: Lippincott, 1968.

Whitehurst, C. A. *Women in America: The oppressed majority*. Pacific Palisades, Cal.: Goodyear, 1977.

Wolfgang, M. E., Savitz, L., & Johnston, J. (Eds.) *The sociology of crime and delinquency*. New York: Wiley, 1962.

Wolfgang, M. E., Savitz, L., & Johnston, J. (Eds.) *The sociology of punishment and correction*. New York: Wiley, 1970.

Wright, R., Richard Wright. In R. Crossmen (Ed.), *The God that failed*. New York: Harper & Row, 1949. Pp. 103–146.

Author Index

Subject Index

DATE DUE

SEP 1 3 1988		
SEP 2 1988		
JUL 2 7 1990		
AUG 2 1 1990		
SEP 1 2 1990		
NOV 4 1991		
DEC 2 2 1991		
APR 7 1992		
APR 2 7 1992		
MAY 2 6 1992		
DEC 1 7 1993		